For my brother
Doug
and my pal
Brian,
two real friends when
I needed them most

The
6
Imperatives
of
Marketing

Lessons From the World's Best Companies

Allan J. Magrath

amacom

American Management Association

This publication is designed to provide accurate and authoritative
information in regard to the subject matter covered. It is sold with the
understanding that the publisher is not engaged in rendering legal,
accounting, or other professional service. If legal advice or other expert
assistance is required, the services of a competent professional person
should be sought.

Library of Congress Cataloging-in-Publication Data

Magrath, Allan J.
       The 6 imperatives of marketing: lessons from the world's
best companies / Allan J. Magrath.
          p.   cm.
     Includes bibliographical references and index.
     ISBN 0-8144-5042-3
     1. Marketing.   2. Consumer satisfaction.   I. Title.
HF5415.122.M34   1992   91-33714
658.8—dc20   CIP

Printing number

10 9 8 7 6 5 4 3 2 1

Contents

Every morning in Africa, a gazelle wakes up. It knows it must run faster than the fastest lion or it will be killed. Every morning a lion wakes up. It knows it must outrun the slowest gazelle or it will starve to death. It doesn't matter whether you are a lion or a gazelle: When the sun comes up, you'd better be running.

—*Unknown*

The
6
Imperatives
of
Marketing

Introduction

Life is lived forward but understood backward.

Kierkegaard

So many changes are occurring in marketing today that executives often find it difficult to sort out the real ducks from the decoys. Which are the crucial lasting issues, and which are passing fads? Which developments must be responded to, learned, and mastered? We live in a time of unprecedented market uncertainty; the order of the day is often disorder. What does a company that seeks marketing leadership need to know—and do?

This book explores the larger issues that any marketing-driven corporation should look at and act upon. "Marketing" is meant in the largest sense of the marketing mission—the business of centering the corporation's efforts around customer needs, so that customers bond to the company, continuing to buy at a profit to the company, in mutually satisfying long-term value exchanges. *In this respect, marketing is everyone's job, not just those with marketing titles on their doors. Marketing is an orientation, not an organization.*

The Changes

The marketing landscape is changing on many levels. On a mega level, new trading blocs and market structures are emerging in Europe, along the Pacific rim, and in the North American Free Trade Zone. Mergers and acquisitions, which are taking place at

1

a feverish pace, are transforming entire industries; the airline industry, for example, is now dominated by a handful of mega-carriers. Privatization is creating new entities from formerly regulated operations, and the collapse of Communist dominance in Eastern Europe is opening up vast new markets with unfilled needs and expectations.

At a micro level, buyer-seller relationships are also undergoing transformations. An increased emphasis on quality control is resulting in buyer-seller partnerships, more sole sourcing, and shared customer-supplier teamwork programs for mutual productivity improvements. The quality concept, including service and customer satisfaction attributes, is coming to embody an augmented notion of products. Milliken & Company epitomizes customer partnering. It sells shop towels to laundries, which in turn supply factories. Milliken commands a 10–15 percent price premium because, in addition to supplying towels, its representatives help their customers with their accounting, truck routing, market research, and even the training of their sales forces. It builds value that goes beyond selling shop towels.

At the front lines of marketing, companies are frequently eschewing mass market campaigns in favor of those aimed at micro markets, in response to an increased range of technologically possible products and the tendency of customers to fragment their tastes. Manufacturers have learned to make a wide variety of goods at competitive costs, something unheard of when mass marketing and long production runs dominated corporate thinking.

The movement of customers into specialized segments is mirrored in retailing, where retailers catering to a specialized clientele and hybrid retailers of all sorts are emerging. There are now stores that market only products for left-handers. In addition, mixed channel systems are growing as consumers and businesses show new eagerness to buy from direct marketers, catalog houses, and other nontraditional trade sources.

Mass media marketing efforts are often supplemented by campaigns in specialized media of all sorts, from point-of-purchase promotions to event sponsorships. In 1989, 584 new magazines, many aimed at specialized readerships, were started in America, more than double the number of 1985 launches; the average American receives seventeen pounds more mail than he or she did ten years ago. So pervasive are these new media that they have spawned a whole new vocabulary, including "junk fax," "advertorials," "infomercials," and "videofax catalogs." Sales promotion activities, including a growing volume of cross-promotions of products or services planned by allied companies, now dwarf branded product ad spending. Further, direct selling methods are less commonly used, while dealers, value-added resellers, agents, distributors, systems integrators, and franchise arrangements are growing in number by leaps and bounds. There are even franchised funeral parlors.

Six Marketing Imperatives

In the midst of this inexorable march of new customers, new competitors, new technologies, and new distribution patterns sits today's executive—intent on finding opportunities amidst discontinuities. Doing so astutely requires an appreciation of which issues are the make-or-break ones to master.

Using more than 300 company examples, I discuss in *The 6 Imperatives of Marketing* the implications of key challenges for a company's marketing orientation. These are the "big-picture" issues that cut across geographic boundaries, customer classifications, and channel networks.

Productivity

The first of the critical six issues is the preservation of profit margins via improvements in productivity. Market-driven companies must accomplish their share goals by containing marketing costs, from sales and customer mix management to clever program choices in trade and end user supports. Market share without margin is profitless prosperity—the hollowest sort of victory—in which no reinvestments are possible in new products, new markets, human resources, and brand franchises. With parity in product performance evident in so many markets, the productivity of marketing spending in nonproduct areas ulti-

mately determines the health of a business's margins and competitive position.

Innovation

A second make-or-break issue is the need to be strongly and
continuously innovative and to understand the value-added dimensions that count most with customers. From this perspective,
marketing-oriented managers can determine optimum positionings and customer needs and then determine the skills and tasks
required to attain optimum value-added connections. Product
innovation is the oxygen that invigorates customers while feeding
the twin fires of growth and profitability.

Distribution Channels

A third concern of market-driven managers is the creation of
durable distribution channel relationships, given the proliferation
of "information-smart," large distribution channels. Wholesaler
middlemen and chain retailers' clout is increasing; with such
channel power shifts comes the need for management to guarantee access to products and services to its end customers. "Share-
of-shelf" retail store battles will be as key in the competition for
end customer brand loyalty as share-of-mind brand recognition
battles. When Hershey bought Cadbury's chocolate brands, it
boosted its total share of shelf past that of its long-time rival,
M&M/Mars, in a move symptomatic of the fight for control of
expensive selling space.

Alliances

A fourth fundamental issue facing marketing executives is the
mastery of acquisitions, comarketing, and alliance-venturing arrangements. As the need for collaborative marketing between
corporations increases and go-it-alone companies become increasingly scarce, market-centered executives will have to learn to
partner well and often in a myriad of alliances from logistics to
selling, advertising, promotion, public relations, and joint distribution. Alliances are the kind of loose-fitting, creativity-tapping

arrangements that suit the fluid environment in which so many companies in so many markets operate today.

Globalization

The fifth big-picture concern is the globalization of products and services. When the number-one selling car in America is the Honda Accord, it is pretty clear that marketing leadership is a global game. It's no longer good enough to be first-class; companies must now be world-class. Market-driven executives must learn what it means to globalize strategies, tactics, operations, and organizations.

Quality

The sixth imperative is to emphasize, nurture, and develop Quality in all marketing practices and approaches. Quality is needed in marketing planning and customer research efforts; it is mandatory in customer responsiveness, from order contact personnel to complaint handling, emergency expedites, on-time delivery, sales rep problem solving, and over forty other elements. Driving quality through a marketing organization requires mastery of analytic tools such as benchmarking and human processes such as empowerment. Quality-obsessed marketing executives can work wonders, as evidenced by the revival of Ford, Motorola, Xerox, and other companies whose people have caught the Quality religion.

Putting It All Together—Rubbermaid, Inc.

Rubbermaid, Inc.,[1] is one of the most admired* corporations in the United States, in large part because it has succeeded in mastering all six of these make-or-break marketing issues. A $1,000 investment in Rubbermaid stock in 1980 would have been worth $18,000 in 1990, if all the dividends had been reinvested.

*Fortune Annual Poll of top executives, outside directors, and financial analysts ranked Rubbermaid number two in 1988 behind Merck & Co., among 306 companies rated. Its ranking was up from 5th in 1987.

Rubbermaid is an extremely disciplined, productivity-minded marketing outfit. Losing businesses, including an in-home party plan company, a low-margin automotive car mat and accessories operation, and price-sensitive "bid"-type businesses such as the sale of municipal trash receptacles, were sold off. Rubbermaid lowered unit costs by reorganizing from eight divisions to five and implementing factory scrap reduction programs and other employee cost-savings suggestions. It typically invests 10 percent of net sales to upgrade and automate equipment and facilities. The result? Even though its prices are 5–10 percent higher than those of its competitors, its net margin of 8.3 percent of sales tops all its competitors, and return on average shareholder's equity moved from 15.2 percent in 1980 to 21.3 percent in 1987.

Rubbermaid's innovation and know-how about adding value with distinction has enabled its new product line to grow to more than 2,000 from a few hundred; Rubbermaid derives 30 percent of its sales from products that have been on the market for less than five years. It is launching a whole new product line of indoor recycling bins to meet the emerging needs of "green" consumers.

Between 1980 and 1988, Rubbermaid doubled its distribution coverage from 60,000 to 120,000 outlets and now partners with its largest key retailers in all sorts of jointly-designed displays, merchandising plans, promotions, and logistics improvements. Rubbermaid believes in seeking win-win solutions with trade channels instead of adopting a "we-they" confrontational mentality and is mastering the intricacies of enhanced market access.

Furthermore, Rubbermaid has shown itself deft at both acquisitions and alliances. It has acquired Little Tykes Toy Company, Gott Corporation (a maker of coolers), Viking Brush, Ltd., SECO Industries (which makes commercial floor care products), and MicroComputer Accessories, Inc. It has integrated them all and expanded each of their individual product portfolios. For instance, Little Tykes made twenty-nine products when it was bought by Rubbermaid in 1984; six years later, it sells more than 117 products, including the best-selling kids' "indoor gym." Rubbermaid has an alliance with Allibert in France to manufacture and market casual outdoor resin furniture and an alliance with the Curver Group of Holland, a leading rubber and plastics housewares manufacturer in Europe.

Rubbermaid has markedly increased its overseas operations from seven locations in France, Germany, Switzerland, Belgium, and Austria in 1980 to twenty-five sites in 1989, including all-new operations in Spain, the United Kingdom, and Italy. It has globalized its products well.

Last, Rubbermaid is quality-obsessed. It has intense market research activities to listen to its customers. Its research and development, manufacturing, marketing, management information systems, finance, and human resources personnel all make periodic retail store checks to be certain they understand customer needs. Product designers from its food service group work in restaurants. Rubbermaid runs a day-care center at its Little Tykes headquarters in order to watch its pre-school-age customers play with its products while offering a service to its working mothers and fathers. Rubbermaid responds rapidly to each and every customer complaint, replacing any of its products free, even after many years of use. It is responsive to customer needs; for instance, it added antistatic chemicals to its plastic housewares when retailers complained that their laundry baskets and garbage cans attracted dust. Rubbermaid believes in robust, quality-designed products that don't break or wear out, and it backs up this belief by using thicker gauge plastic and only the best quality resins (never scrap resin). Multi-function quality project teams operate inside business units and are compensated to build strong Rubbermaid brand franchises, thus tying quality to team success and the recognition of business unit managers who manage brand franchises wisely. Rubbermaid's recycling containers for consumers are of such high quality that they are the standard in many towns and cities across North America.

Rubbermaid is a shining example of a company with its eye on the ball, emphasizing the six critical make-or-break issues vital for a successful market-driven corporation in the 1990s.

The six imperatives of marketing are extensively explored in this book, with examples of products and services from companies in more than forty industries. I hope that the illumination of these marketing imperatives can assist executives in drafting their agendas for marketing change—the kind of change that is proactive, positive, and worthy of their energies and talents.

Notes

1. For an extensive write-up on Rubbermaid, see James Braham, "The Billion-Dollar Dustpan," *Industry Week* (August 1, 1988), pp. 46–48; Maria Mallory, "Profits on Everything but the Kitchen Sink," *Business Week*, Special Issue on Innovation (1989), p. 122. See also a speech by Stanley C. Gault, CEO of Rubbermaid, to the Conference Board of Canada, March 29, 1990, Fifteenth Annual Marketing Conference, Toronto, Ontario, Canada.

1

Marketing Productivity: Leveraging Marketing Assets, Spending, and Processes

Ruth made a big mistake when he gave up pitching.

Tris Speaker
Manager, Cleveland Indians Baseball Club, 1921

Raising the Standard in Productivity Attainment

As a pitcher, Babe Ruth was tremendously productive. He was among the American League's "winningest" pitchers, had a strong arm, was a solid nine-inning finisher, and had a respectable number of strikeouts per game. All and all, he was a fine asset to his team.

But productivity is all relative. For while Ruth was a very fine pitcher, he was a *great* hitter. In this regard his productivity was almost unparalleled. He could, and did, win games with a single swing of his bat. With his season totals for home runs, runs batted in, on-base percentage, and home runs over his career, Ruth boosted the fortunes of the New York Yankees as no other player before him. His productivity went beyond winning games—he made the team a success, drew fans in the millions, and was a large part of the reason for the huge expansion of

Yankee Stadium. It isn't called "the house that Ruth built" for nothing.

Marketing managers must learn to look at marketing productivity in the same light as that in which historians look at Babe Ruth's productivity. What was good enough during the 1970s and 1980s is not good enough in a relative sense for the 1990s. Being very good at something (as Ruth was at pitching) is no longer the standard to strive for. Marketing has to leverage its assets to the absolute fullest, as the Yankees did when they took Ruth off the mound and put him into the field and the cleanup part of their batting lineup.

What Is Productivity?

Productivity is the process that underlies the wealth creation function of a business. Businesses that grow, sustain profits, provide excellent returns to shareholders, and dominate their markets are productive. They do more with less—or more with their potential than their peers do with theirs. In this respect, high productivity usually denotes excellent competitiveness.

In manufacturing, productivity is often measured by comparing key outputs to key inputs. That is, sales per employee over time or units of production produced are compared with labor expense or total operating dollars expended. Any number of measurements may suffice to show the relationship between what is sought (sales, profits, output produced, new products launched) and the key resources that had to be expended to obtain these outputs (labor, hours, capital invested, energy consumed, people employed). For example, the minimill Birmingham Steel Corporation is able to achieve outstanding productivity because it can produce a ton of steel with only about a third of the labor required by a competitive megamill.

Over time, if a company's key outputs per key inputs increase faster than those at rival companies, the enterprise will thrive. It will be able to finance itself with its own internally generated funds, pay dividends to shareholders, invest in new technologies in order to remain on top, and benefit other stakeholders such as employees, government (in the form of taxes), unions, suppliers, and the communities in which it does business.

In service industries, productivity is often measured by service indices, such as passengers flown per operating expense (airlines) or insurance claims processed per employee (casualty insurance). In every case, the monitored output is at the heart of the service; the input monitored is often the cost that is largest, called the key cost. For example, in a service business such as retailing, sales per square foot of retail selling space is the index used because retailing is "fixed-asset intensive" (that is, its major assets are in retail locations, fixtures, bricks and mortar versus "liquid assets," such as cash or receivables). By comparison, in a distributor business such as wholesaling, productivity is likely to be based on gross margin dollars earned per employee because wholesaling views itself as producing trading profits as a middleman compared to its key cost, which is often its payroll cost derived from its head count.

Productivity and Marketing

In marketing, productivity is usually measured by sales per input cost, such as the cost of selling, distribution, advertising, or promotion, or some other indicator of overall marketing health. For a company such as 3M, which is innovation-oriented, this indicator could be new product sales as a percentage of total sales accumulated over time. So part of 3M's marketing productivity is monitored according to its sales from new products introduced in the previous five years as a percentage of total sales. This allows 3M to gauge whether its new product innovation yield in marketing is rising, waning, or staying the same. It can compare this ratio to its research and development spending as a percentage of sales to determine if its outputs (new product sales ratios) are being affected by its key input (spending to discover or develop new products in its labs).

Marketing productivity clearly involves either wiser P&L spending by task* or a more productive sales response from equal

---

*P&L means profit and loss expense item; *tasks* relates to selling, promoting, pricing, distributing, and servicing after-sale and other support activities connected to marketing in a company.

spending (or both). In addition, productive marketing organizations *leverage* not only operating expense items (for instance, sales force spending) but also balance sheet items that tie up scarce hard assets (such as inventories, receivables, warehouses, delivery fleets, showrooms, sales branches, or computer systems). (Leverage is the process of boosting bottom-line profits higher through the selective use of fixed assets or operating investments.) There are also less tangible but nevertheless real assets, such as brands, trademarks, logos, patents, customer goodwill, distributor relationships, and the reputation or image of the company in the eyes of target buyers, influencers, and decision makers.

The concept of examining marketing for productivity improvement target areas is illustrated in Figure 1-1.

Productivity in Marketing Strategy

Some marketing strategies are simply more productive than others, in the sense of winning over customers or competitors with the least cost and the greatest exploitation of unique strengths and specialized resources.

In military parlance, productive strategies are those that combine efficiency of effort with concentration of force. When focused and efficient strategies involve surprise or innovation, competitors much larger in size or resources can often be beaten. Carefully focused strategies enabled Polaroid to win in the instant photography area despite the presence of its much larger rival, Kodak, and helped Compaq Computer to grow quickly despite competition from International Business Machines (IBM), Apple, Digital Equipment, and Hewlett-Packard.

The several variants of productive strategies include:

- Exploiting proprietary advantages that rivals do not have and cannot obtain, such as access to scarce raw materials, low-cost financing, or patented technologies or processes
- Leveraging superior knowledge of customer needs or segments and satisfying them in unique ways before others can

(*text continues on page 14*)

Figure 1-1. Productivity target areas.

1. **Marketing Strategy—Is it productive?**

2. **P&L Spending Areas—Are these tactics all optimally productive?**

Sales Force Spending including
$\begin{cases} \text{Sales Force Administration} \\ \text{Sales Force Operation} \end{cases}$

Advertising Spending (especially branding activities)
Promotional Spending
New Product Activity Spending (including Patents)
Market Research Spending
Packaging Spending
Merchandising/Pricing Program Spending
Physical Distribution Spending
Distributor/Dealer/Retailer Program Spending

3. **Balance Sheet Asset Areas—Are all real or intangible assets optimally leveraged? (for maximum sales, margins, or market share)?**

Real Assets	Intangible Assets
Inventories	Patents
Receivables	Brands
Sales Offices	Trademarks
Warehouses	Customer Information/Goodwill
Store Locations	Satisfaction/Retention Rate
Fleets	Dealer Networks and
Fixtures	Relationships
Computers/Sales Technologies	Image/Reputation
Telecommunications	Morale, Helpfulness, Skill of
Ordering Systems	Front-Line Customer Contact
	Personnel
	Management Skill

- Venturing with partners in ways that provide for synergy in resource sharing
- Outsourcing or spinning off operations in order to free up capital, people, and other assets that can be put to a more productive use
- Exploiting advantages of *scale* inherent in areas such as manufacturing processes, volume buying of critical cost components, operating systems, or utilizing machinery
- Exploiting economics of *scope* inherent in finding ways to connect wide product assortments and broad customer bases, with a view to bonding more tightly to distributor or end customers

Proprietary Advantages

Patents or investments in proprietary advantages exclusive to a company represent sunk costs. When a company can exploit such advantages to the fullest, great productivity results, enhancing returns on sales and on equity.

Consider Catalina Marketing of Anaheim, California, a company with a patented system for distributing coupons to food shoppers based on actual scanned purchases. Because Catalina's equipment is the only patented system of its kind* and because the benefits of this type of coupon dispensing are very high, it has been able to place 3,000 units in U.S. stores in a very short time.

Owens-Illinois of Toledo has sunk costs in the most state-of-the-art glass container manufacturing processes in the world. As a result, it is a highly productive competitor, despite the commodity nature of its business in pickle, beer, and beverage bottles and jars.

Safeway, Inc., the privately owned supermarket giant headquartered in Oakland, California, has invested heavily in computerized inventory control systems and point-of-sale scanner systems. Safeway exploits this technology not only to help it run its

*Catalina's design allows a manufacturer to tailor a coupon program precisely to a consumer's shopping basket; coupon offers can be triggered by the purchase of a complementary product or of a competitor's or a like product in a different size or flavor.

stores efficiently but to sell its information systems to manufacturers, who pay Safeway to tap its knowledge of shopper habits. For instance, Procter & Gamble pays Safeway to conduct in-store tests to determine which method of on-shelf packaging and display generates the biggest sales per square foot. Procter & Gamble increased bar soap sales 5 percent when it discovered from Safeway's database of customer knowledge that its hand soaps sold better stacked on the shelf than from a wire dump bin display.[1] Productivity from an information investment strategy has a huge payoff for a company such as Safeway, where a half of a one percent shift in margin equals $7 million in net profit.

Superior Customer Knowledge

Segmenting customers more cleverly than competitors and using segmentation knowledge to serve customers uniquely has tremendous productivity benefits. Money is saved because the selection of prospects ensures that only good sales candidates are targeted. Once potential buyers have been targeted, a variety of research techniques, including supermarket scanners, can help the company understand how its promotions directly affect sales response. This can help fine-tune offers by geographic area or customer type.

Ocean Spray Cranberries, Inc., moved sales from just over $100 million in the mid 1970s to over $750 million by 1990 with such a marketing strategy. Loctite[2] (anaerobic adhesives), Porsche (sports cars), Compaq (small computers), Robert Bosch (automotive lighting), and Maytag (household appliances) are all fine examples of companies whose productivity is high because their superior knowledge of specialized customers allows them to exploit niches in markets.

Focusing on a select group or target number of customers concentrates a business's spending for maximum results. For instance, Bodine Corporation of Bridgeport, Connecticut, builds specialized high-speed machinery for manufacturers to use on their assembly lines. Bodine's machines help Champion assemble spark plugs, Sony load videocassettes, and General Electric manufacture alkaline batteries. Bodine makes only thirty machines a year, but each one sells for over $1 million. Bodine continues to thrive, as it has for almost sixty years (since 1933). It is in a small market niche, but it is so focused on its customers' needs that it can deliver superior value while earning a nice return on all of its engineering efforts.

Hemmings Motor News of Bennington, Vermont, thrives in a publishing business dominated by a few huge companies. A publisher of ads for antique and vintage cars and auto parts directed to hobbyists and car collectors, Hemmings's niche strategy has paid off in tremendous productivity. With 297,000 paid subscribers, it has sales of $20 million and profits close to $4 million, and its growth is in excess of 10 percent per year. Its productivity per employee is quite amazing, since all of its sales and profits are earned by only eighty employees. It *never* discounts its prices, and it's been doing business this way for twenty-two years.

Niche strategies work productively even in industries dominated by big players, such as publishing or consumer packaged goods. For instance, Warner Lambert is a niche player in some seventeen different categories of consumer goods. Its brands (which include Halls' cough drops, Rolaids antacids, Trident sugarless gum, Benadryl cough medicine, and Listerine mouthwash) have number-one or number-two market shares in their respective market niches, despite the presence of giant dominant competitors such as Procter & Gamble and Wrigley Gum.

Joint Ventures

When companies share costs and risks in a joint venture, the payoff is often disproportionately productive for both. For instance, Inland Steel of Chicago and Nippon Steel of Japan jointly own I/N Tek, a 200-acre plant in New Carlisle, Indiana. This factory contains the latest technology for turning 65- by ⅛-inch steel coils into flattened, shaped, and treated flat-rolled sheets for use as auto hoods, refrigerator doors, and office furniture panels. The process is a three-mile–long continuous one that turns out a sheet in one hour, compared to the twelve days required with the old technology of cold rolling. Through its partnership with Nippon, Inland was able to gain access to the newest technology (owned by Nippon), as well as access to Japanese customers such as Honda and Toyota for some of the factory's output. Because the plant's costs are the lowest for cold rolling mills in America and because its output is of such high quality, Inland commands a price premium for its sales that is 25 to 40 percent higher than that for standard commodity steel products. What about productivity? In the words of Inland's president, "Without casting one more ton of steel, Inland boosted its profits by $200 million"[3]; its steel now generates $100 a ton in operating profits compared with $60 per ton in 1988. This joint venture has been so productive that Inland and Nippon are expanding their shared cost partnership to include a new galvanizing plant to cost $450 million in 1991–1992.

Joint ventures frequently result in big productivity gains in marketing. A joint venture between Heinz and the People's Republic of China originally began producing baby food products but is not expanding into soups and ketchup. Dow Chemical's 1990 joint venture with Eli Lilly on agricultural chemicals has resulted in a $1.5 billion powerhouse, now the world's fifth largest supplier of such chemicals.[4]

Joint ventures create synergies that often expand sales faster than costs. They also leverage assets at a rate far in excess of what alternative investments could produce with the same dollars.

Outsourcing or Divestiture

When companies shed operations that represent a drag on their competitiveness (or that tie up resources that could produce better returns elsewhere), they boost their productivity. Gerber has done much better since spinning off those of its businesses not related to baby food. Coca-Cola divested itself of its nonbeverage businesses, such as a wine subsidiary and its 49 percent stake in Columbia Pictures, and invested the proceeds in overseas expansion, which has been very successful; in 1985 operating income from overseas contributed 53 percent of Coke's total corporate operating profits, compared with 77 percent in 1989. Return on equity from these overseas investments is 38 percent, and Coke's market share is way up in both growing nations such as Taiwan and mature nations such as France. Heinz "dispassionately" spins off businesses in which it is not winning and that are dragging down its productivity of capital. For example, it recently sold Robs Restaurants and Stanley Wine, two Australian companies that it believed were tying up scarce resources better used elsewhere.[5] Colgate-Palmolive has done much better without its health care operations, concentrating instead on its consumer and industrial products.

Many specialized marketing services are outsourced because the cost of providing them in-house would not be competitive on a "productivity for dollars expended" basis. The services of advertising agencies, trade-show booth designers, packaging consultants, public relations firms, sales promotion houses, graphic designers, premium and incentive specialists, audio-visual production houses, market research agencies, and direct marketing experts are examples of pools of talented outsiders better hired by the project, task, hour, or campaign. To carry the fixed costs associated with having such specialized resources on staff when their productive use is often variable doesn't make economic sense.

It may also make sense to outsource functions that support marketing and selling when the service provided can be proven reliable, credible, and cost competitive. For example, capable sales training personnel are usually available for spot duty to train a company's reps or its distributor reps for very competitive rates per session. Often, such trainers specialize by topic, such as negotiating, time-territory planning, selling skills, key account management skills, and listening skills.

Outsourcing marketing or any support service better or equally performed at less (or equivalent) cost elsewhere allows a company to concentrate on its unique talents. For instance, Kodak retains IBM to manage its corporate data center so it can concentrate on marketing and refining its imaging technologies. In so doing, Kodak frees up capital, space, time, and talents better employed elsewhere applying fast-breaking information technology to help its business unit managers. In point of fact, even including IBM's fee to manage Kodak's data center, Kodak has cut its annual cost for this function by close to 50 percent compared with the cost of doing it in-house.

Exploiting Scale Advantages

For a great many businesses, it pays to be big or to manage plant capacity with more success than rivals. In the airline, credit card, and telecommunications industries, the advantages of scale are major. That is why there are only a handful of mega-carriers left in the United States, why only a few credit cards (Visa, Master-Card, American Express) dominate worldwide usage, and why AT&T and other telecommunication giants still dominate their markets despite rivals who have taken a run at them (GTE-Sprint and MCI).

Increased size does not always lead to the lowest unit cost, as it once did; more and more, productivity in strategy demands astute decision making related to plant capacity additions and shutdowns. Companies in process industries such as meat packing, corrugated packaging, chemicals, and steel that can tune their capacity utilization by astutely closing marginal high-cost plants while adding or retrofitting other lower-cost plants can be sure-fire winners; they have high productivity and low costs because they are so good at balancing factory capacity investments to market opportunity, all the while assuring themselves that they can maintain superior cost positions relative to rivals. Nucor Corporation in Charlotte, North Carolina, has grown from sales of $120 million as a steel maker in 1960 to a billion dollars in sales by pursuing such a productive strategy. Stone Container Corporation, a market leader in corrugated packaging, not only balances its total factory network capacity against market opportunity, it is the best in its industry at figuring out what type and degree of automation make sense for each of its factories.[6]

American Express is a fine example of a company that has exploited the high fixed costs of maintaining a huge marketing database and customer file on credit card users and buying preferences. By utilizing its system, American Express has been able to expand and promote a greater variety of products and services to its cardholders (such as insurance) and to upgrade cardholders to higher value (status) cards as a way to increase revenues per card at little incremental cost in card acquisition or account servicing. In return, holders of high-status (gold) cards receive differentiated services such as year-end summaries of purchases organized by expense category, which are useful in preparing tax returns.

One of the purest marketing-driven businesses in the world—advertising—has undergone a shakeout and consolidation. Scale in this particular industry pays off in three ways. Larger agencies can negotiate more powerfully with media giants, such as Time-Warner, for the best volume buys on media placements; they can service clients around the world, regardless of country; and they can coordinate campaigns in multiple countries to ensure that a consistent image and message emerge while minimizing duplication of creative material. This last factor is becoming increasingly important with the growth of global event marketing, such as Olympic or World Cup soccer and skiing sponsorships.

Economies of Scope

Huffy Corporation, founded in 1928 near Dayton, Ohio, is well known as the last remaining 100 percent domestically-owned manufacturer of bicycles in the United States. It has the largest share of the American bike market, and its plant in Celina, Ohio, is one of the most productive anywhere; in fact, it has the lowest man-hours per bicycle among worldwide bike producers. But Huffy also has an excellent little business called YLC Enterprises, which it started as a way to exploit one of its economies of scope—low-cost access to retail customers.

Huffy sells its bikes to retailers such as Kmart on an unassembled basis. Its managers recognized that if the company's customers wanted to sell the bikes already assembled, perhaps Huffy could build the bikes for the retailers who already sold its unassembled bikes. Its retail accounts enthusiastically endorsed this idea, because it allowed them to market assembled bicycles to the public on the same basis as smaller bicycle shops, despite their mass-merchant orientation. Huffy has pushed this economy of scope even further by offering to set up other companies' products, which the retailers buy unassembled but want to sell assembled or to display in a setup condition in the store. Huffy's YLC Enterprises sets up knockdown furniture, barbeque grills, lawn mowers, exercise equipment, and gym sets and even assembles store displays for its "Kmart-type" customers.

Exploiting an economy of scope based on product line range or common customers between divisions is not the only type of strategy in which a high productivity payoff is apparent. Often, a company's best economy of scope is its broad distribution coverage, or contacts.

Heinz has made a series of strategic European acquisitions specifically designed to exploit its distribution coverage throughout the continent. For example, Heinz bought Spain's leading fried tomato (tomato frito) producer because it could combine the producer with its tomato solids operation in Portugal and, using the same distribution setup in both countries, expand market share for each basic product. Heinz, like most food producers, often exploits scope economies in advertising by launching multiple brand promotions with large retailers in which Heinz products in a variety of categories are featured. These might include ketchup, Heinz's Ore-Ida frozen french fries, Heinz's Nine-Lives Cat Food, and Heinz pickles, BBQ sauce, or baked beans. By pulling its multiple brands together in joint ad features, Heinz can exploit its economies in key account selling and co-op advertising.

Farmer Brothers, the $200 million (annual gross sales) coffee supplier to restaurants, exploits its distribution system very cleverly. Since it sends a truck to deliver coffee to customers weekly anyway, it has added some 200 other restaurant supply items, from Styrofoam cups to spices, on such deliveries. Clever exploitation of its delivery system has resulted in $40 million in added sales per year.

3M has a variety of market-based marketing organizations, such as its automotive center in Detroit, in which multiple 3M divisions pool resources to sell to or develop products for common customers. If customers are shared by two businesses, joint venture scope economies are also possible. For example, Kodak exposes Disney cartoon characters such as Mickey Mouse in its ads in return for exclusive rights to market its film at Disney's amusement parks. This fifteen-year agreement exploits the synergy that exists between both companies' customers.

Tactical Marketing Productivity

While having the right strategy in and of itself can be a productivity booster, tactics are often the difference between also-ran and outstanding marketing companies. Continental Cablevision of Boston has the highest productivity among American cable operators. Sixty percent of its customers buy its premium services (compared to the industry average of 40 percent), and it loses only 2.2 percent of its customers a year from discontinued service (the industry loses 3 percent on average).

Continental Cablevision is considered its industry's best marketing company. Why? It isn't so much Continental's strategy that differs (all cable operators try to sell premium services and hold down customer turnover), but its tactics. It is the smartest in the business at using advanced direct marketing techniques, from door-to-door sales to direct mail and telemarketing. Its tactical proficiency at boosting its top line simply exceeds that of other cable operators.

Tactical productivity in marketing doesn't mean only getting a stronger top line sales boost from certain forms of marketing spending. It also means "spending sharp" by doing more or the same with less money. Spending efficiency is critical today because an average diversified manufacturing company needs 10–15 percent before-tax profit just to survive; it needs twice this level if half of its profits are paid out in dividends to shareholders. Failure to achieve these pre-tax targets means that growth in competition with rivals cannot be self-financed, even if all earnings are retained in the business. And a failure to grow can lead to lost market share, an unfavorable relative cost position, and a permanent negative cash flow. Astute marketing spending is vital for any business that wants to avoid heavy fixed debt obligations and to pursue available growth opportunities. Another reason cost control in marketing tactics is so vital is that many businesses do not control market prices and must therefore control spending if they are to prosper, or even survive, if prices drop.

Phelps Dodge Corporation, a copper producer, lost $400 million in 1983. In 1989 it had record profits on $2.3 billion in sales. How did this happen? Phelps Dodge learned to make copper for sixty-five cents a pound from eighty-five cents in 1984 because copper prices plummeted and it could not boost the prices it charged for this worldwide traded commodity. Phelps Dodge learned how to cut costs and turn a profit *regardless* of copper's sagging price.[7]

One of the keys in managing costs is to avoid overspending during a heady growth phase that can hurt later on when the business cycle cools off. Customers, investors, and employees bring tremendous pressure to bear on spending during market upturns because they want a company to take full advantage of opportunities during the boom. However, booms don't last, and dangerous overexpansion can set the scene for a disaster when the economic upturn plays itself out. An example of the danger of overexpansion is the U.S. hotel industry. The travel boom of the 1980s is over; the hotel building boom of that period continued too long, resulting in overcapacity, losses of $350 million by hotel chains in the United States, and a record 314 properties driven into bankruptcy in 1990.[8] Sound spending practices dictate holding back on some irreversible decisions in the growth phase to avoid disaster when the bubble bursts (which it inevitably does). Companies can choose to rent rather than lease, for example, or to lease instead of buy or to buy with the possibility of future sale. Caution in capital additions is called for, and using subcontractors may be a better way of meeting short-term demand than taking on a lot of new staff or developing new support functions within the company. Similarly, a company might avoid building excessive inventories and instead prune marginal lines and slow movers, freeing up capital and capacity without damaging service levels or production on fast movers. Purchase contracts should be kept short unless low cancellation charges can be negotiated on long ones. Sensible cost containment practices and the liquidation of unused assets can keep a company from having to make desperation cuts if recession strikes or hard-pressed competition gets tougher. The most commonsense attitude about marketing spending was summed up by Heinz CEO Tony O'Reilly, who said: "We feel the spear of the marketplace in our back. . . . All it takes is modest shortfall in volume or a modest hiccup in cost control and we become exposed to earnings loss very quickly. . . . [W]e are extremely conscious of the vulnerability of even our greatest brands."[9]

Product Line Management Strategies

Patent Productivity

Companies can employ a number of tactics to leverage up on sunk product development costs. DuPont provides a fine example of how to boost the sales of an older product, even one whose patent has expired.[10]

In 1959, DuPont invented Lycra, a superstretch polymer originally sold for the manufacture of girdles. Through astute selling, DuPont moved the sale of Lycra (generically referred to as spandex) from girdles in the 1960s to bathing suits in the 1970s and bicyclists' pants and aerobic outfits in the 1980s. In the 1990s, DuPont has made a mass market breakthrough with Lycra by selling its application for new body-hugging designer outfits in cashmere, velour, and velvet combinations. Working with cotton textile manufacturers, DuPont has developed a cotton-Lycra blend that is very delicate and that is today being sold for dresses, pants, shirts, and leggings sold at stores from Kmart to Bloomingdale's; DuPont's sales have grown to $840 million a year, with $210 million of this pure operating profit.

DuPont's clever marketing has allowed for high productivity from a very old product (Lycra is more than thirty years old). By continuously improving the product for expanded applications, DuPont has found a way to sell the benefits of this fiber, which is wrinkle-free and which retains its shape, to several more generations of women. Many companies give up on products after their initial life cycle sales appear to have plateaued. Expanding a product's use by continuous refinement or adaptation is a much smarter productivity move. Himont, Inc., the joint venture specialty chemical manufacturer formed by Hercules, Inc., and Montedison SpA of Italy, grew from $15 million in sales and 8 percent after-tax profits in 1984 to $1.7 billion in sales and 22 percent after-tax profits in 1988 by finding multiple uses for its polypropylene, which is now used in more than 250 new applications where it has replaced less versatile, more expensive plastics. Himont has sold polypro since 1983 for use in tents, sewer pipes, see-through juice bottles, VCR tape boxes, carpet fibers, car bumpers, disposable diapers, and even plastic syringes for hospitals. Not bad for a product invented in 1954.

Maximizing the Mix

Another productive product line tactic involves paying special attention to the sales mix of items sold. AMP is the world's leading manufacturer of connectors because it dominates the distribution of connectors with more variations, constructions, and market niche coverage. Similarly, Walgreen Company outshines all other major drugstore chains in growth and profits and ranks high on the list of all U.S. retailers (including the likes of Toys "R" Us and Nordstrom). How does it do this? By managing its product mix more skillfully than others in its industry. Walgreen uses its high-margin prescription drug business as a traffic builder and then convinces its shoppers to load up on most of the items you can buy at a convenience store (snacks, milk, bread, frozen dinners) plus items you used to find at the old five-and-dime variety store (shampoo, cosmetics, greeting cards, camera film, electric fans, glassware, and even luggage). To this list can also be added traditional drugstore items such as vitamins, pregnancy test kits, and diapers. As a result, an average purchase is $9 at Walgreen, compared with $2.50 at a convenience store or $6 at competitive drugstores.

Managing for maximum order size is a solid productivity practice; after the customer has been drawn to the store for a planned purchase, impulse items are then added on at no incremental advertising cost. In manufacturing, incremental add-on sales usually call for product line spin-offs that augment the core offering. Mattel's core "cash cow" product line is Barbie, the perky queen of dolls, who has been on the market more than thirty years. Barbie spin-offs include Barbie fashions, cars, vans, houses, an airplane, a health club, a ski chalet, a mansion, and other Barbie doll family members (boyfriend Ken, little sister Skipper, and even a Hispanic version of Barbie named Teresa). What's the total effect of spin-off sales? Over $700 million in Barbie and its spin-offs in 1990, up from $430 million in 1987 three years before.[11]

This same strategy of product line offshoots and expanded

choice has allowed Marvin Lumber and Cedar, Inc., to become the fastest-growing producer of windows and doors in the United States. In 1989 Marvin's sales were approximately $265 million, up from $40 million in 1979, as a result of offering more sizes, shapes, and types of windows and doors than its competitors. So great is Marvin's range of products that its price book is two inches thick. Its product selection is two to three times that of its main rivals, Andersen and Pella. Clearly, clever line extensions, whether in kids' dolls or windows and doors, can boost the top line and carve out enviable market shares for an astute user of this tactic.

Augmenting Product With Service

Another productivity tactic is to boost a product's attractiveness by combining it with a service. Home Depot, America's largest home repair chain, has built a very strong business by hiring former electricians, carpenters, plumbers, and other tradesmen to sell its fix-it supplies. Customers flock to Home Depot stores because the sales clerks there really do add value. They know how to build decks, fences, and rec rooms and can offer advice on topics from choice of materials to methods of construction. Home Depot's sales have grown to $2.7 billion with a tidy profit of $112 million as a result of linking product with service.

When Jaguar sells its luxury XJR-S sports car for more than $62,000, it offers a three-and-a-half day course to teach owners to drive it for maximum pleasure for another $1,700. Now that's value added service!

In its own way, industrial electronics distributor Anthem Electronics does the same thing Jaguar does. It used to supply only electronic parts to industrial high-tech accounts. Today it either sells the parts on a freestanding basis or takes the customers' parts list, buys the parts, tests them, assembles them, and sells them to the customer as finished components. The result of more value added service? Sales are growing 21 percent a year, and profits on its $319 million in sales (1989) are at 4.9 percent, despite competitors who often have net profits of 2 percent or less in a cutthroat, thin-margin industry.[12]

Given that product line costs usually represent the largest

single expenditure on the P&L, productivity in augmenting sales with service, spin-offs, line extensions, or new applications is not much good without the ability to manufacture on a cost-competitive basis. Rubbermaid, despite its many successful new products and line extensions, remains committed to being the low-cost producer among its competitors. Himont, which has worked wonders finding new uses for polypropylene, is successful on the bottom line only because it manufactures a pound of polypropylene for 20 percent less than its rivals can.[13]

Even Mattel, which cranks out 54,000 Barbie dolls a day, has had to make a concerted effort to watch costs closely. Mattel's chairman slashed the workforce 22 percent in 1989 and closed ten of Mattel's least productive factories to stay competitive in manufacturing dolls and other toys. Walgreen can boost sales per customer with a large product assortment mix only by using the most sophisticated inventory control system among drug chains in order to control the costs and risks inherent in selling so many different items; otherwise, slow-moving stock write-downs might nullify any sales gain impacts on its profits. AMP is its industry's toughest low-cost competitor despite its huge product assortment.

Productivity in Selling and Distribution

Selling and distribution costs are usually the largest area of marketing spending in which to seek leverage, after product costs. In fact, the efficiency with which gross margin dollars are spent is often a function of the spending efficiency of a company's distribution system and sales force management.

In seeking to boost productivity from these two spending areas, managements can employ a variety of ideas. Low-cost indirect channels such as dealers, distributors, agents, catalogers, or other forms of channels can supplement or substitute for high-cost direct selling channels. The trade-off in moving to indirect channels is that broader market coverage often can be attained at more affordable costs at the cost of relinquishing some degree of control, since intermediaries are less easily directed than a company's own sales personnel. The use of telephone sales solicitations instead of face-to-face sales visits can also contain costs while still yielding excellent results. Thorm-A-Stor, the United Kingdom's fastest-growing window manufacturer, uses inside teleselling extensively to prospect for new customers. It then closes on these prospects, using outside sales reps who call on prospects in person. Its 300-person telesales force has helped build Thorm-A-Stor into the third largest company in the United Kingdom in what is a very crowded fragmented industry.[14] A great many distributor businesses use inside telesales personnel, and they have had outstanding results with this less costly sales method than with traditional outside on-the-road reps.

Using Sales Time for Greatest Productivity

While altering sales channels can boost productivity, the biggest factor holding down sales productivity improvements has been the inability of many companies to make better use of sales reps' time.

Sales & Marketing Management magazine tracked sales productivity from 1977 to 1987 and found that sales volume per rep, after discounting for price inflation (that is, looking only at unit productivity), had only gone up .9 percent a year.[15] Yet the costs of selling have risen relentlessly in terms of hotel room rates, air fares, auto expenses, the costs of meals and entertaining customers, and accompanying costs for sales aids, literature, product samples, brochures, and presentation materials (audio-visual kits, videotapes, and sound-slide shows). Meager productivity gains at many companies are the result of an inability to boost the percentage of reps' time spent engaged in actual selling, face-to-face with customers.

Figure 1-2 (derived from cross-industry survey data) shows how reps spend their time. Actual face-to-face sales time represents less than one-third of total rep time; the balance is spent in internal meetings, training sessions, travelling, or doing paperwork.

Businesses are attempting all sorts of productivity initiatives to cut nonselling time, from scheduling fewer meetings to trying to train reps via videotape, self-study, and other after-selling-hour techniques. Paperwork reduction schemes are also being

Figure 1-2. Sales force time by activity (1990 U.S. cross-industry average).

Source: Data adapated from *Sales & Marketing Management*'s 1990 annual survey of selling costs.

aggressively pursued; examples are the use of faster, more on-line, less paper-intensive systems such as laptops computers, cellular phones, and facsimile. Often such systems can speed written customer proposal or presentation preparations and give reps more responsive supports on price quotes or product specification/application questions. Some software allows reps to redo customer proposals on laptops right in the customer's office in order to customize sales presentations more closely to the customer's particular needs. The insurance industry, for example, uses this technique extensively. But getting reps to sell "smarter" often calls for more than technology or administrative support system investments. Frequently, smarter selling requires entirely new rep skills, direction, and emphasis. The four most common productivity programs aimed at getting more revenue for the limited amount of face-to-face selling possible are:

1. Team selling
2. "Specialization" selling
3. Seminar selling
4. Partnering with customers (often termed relationship management)

Team selling requires reps to team up with distributor and dealer reps to go after target accounts together. Reps may also team with other functional specialists in the company, from tech service reps to manufacturing or customer service personnel, who may each play a major role in helping large key accounts achieve a satisfactory solution for their needs. IBM, for example, teams with the reps of their value-added remarketers, while DuPont often uses multifunction teams to call on key accounts. Each of these techniques is aimed at leveraging more revenue from accounts felt to have large enough potential to justify such team selling investments. Lotus Development Corporation uses two-person teams comprised of a salesperson and a systems engineer to sell new software that requires sophisticated customer education.

The second productivity tactic requires reorganizing a sales force in order to develop industry or market specialists, product specialists, or account specialists. For instance, when General Electric landed the contract for all of General Motors' new Saturn Division's electrical needs, it used specialists from several of its divisions, pulled together by a General Electric senior sales executive—in effect, a collection of specialists steeped in product knowledge and account knowledge about General Motors' key buyers, specifiers, and so on.

Specialization in selling often allows a company to develop in-depth know-how about its customers' businesses so that it can really help its customers' productivity. For example, Edward Don & Company of North Riverside, Illinois, manages a wholesaling business in restaurant supplies (the company operates a 240,000-square-foot warehouse). Its chairman, Robert Don, actively encourages his sales force to work with the company's restaurant customers in order to help them economize on their purchases. He will, if customers require it, go back and negotiate better prices with his suppliers on their behalf as a way to survive in tough times. Don's people can perform this kind of problem-solving "ombudsman" role for their restaurant customers only because of their intimate knowledge of the pressures and concerns of those in the hospitality industry.[16]

Seminar selling, selling customers in groups rather than one by one, is a boost to the productivity of a sales organization. 3M, for instance, sells groups of engineers on the benefits of using micrographic systems for blueprint storage, retrieval, and archival records. Engineers from different firms or from different parts of a large firm can mix as a peer group; in so doing, they often learn from one another, in addition to listening to a 3M expert discuss micrographic systems. For these types of seminars to work, they must be heavily educational in content (selling concepts and applications) and must avoid product sales pitches, since the intended audience usually comprises purchase influencers, rather than purchasing personnel (who may attend the seminars as part of their effort to stay abreast of technology for their profession). After generating interest at a seminar, the company can then make sales presentations to potential customers on an individual basis.

The fourth technique, customer partnering, also produces sales productivity gains. As a result of tight customer linkages at various levels and functions between a supplier and its customer, as the customer's business grows, so too does that of its key supplier. Ultimate customer partnering often involves both the supplier's quality team and its customer's quality team sharing members who exchange specifications, and, often, confidential information about markets and the evolution of new needs and their effect on future product designs. TRW developed such a partnering relationship with Ford on electronic componentry and systems for Ford automobiles and trucks, and a great many software companies have similar strong partnerships with the key original equipment hardware suppliers (such as IBM, Digital Equipment, Apple, and Hewlett-Packard). Any partnering linkages include cross-functional involvement as well as contacts between senior-, middle-, and lower-level management personnel. For instance, as the sales volume of the large disposable diaper manufacturers such as Procter & Gamble and Kimberly Clark has grown, so has the sales volume and global market share of supplier partners such as 3M (which manufactures diaper fastening systems).

All of these sales productivity approaches use two overriding principles—teamwork to serve customers and focused selling. Teamwork boosts productivity because when a team assumes ownership of special accounts, both team problem solving and team suggestions for improvement often follow.[17] Focus in selling assures a company that resources are not wastefully dispersed. Concentrating a company's selling force can often secure market niches in industries dominated by giants. For example, Akzo Engineering Plastics (the U.S. subsidiary of AKZO, N.V. of Holland), located in Evansville, Indiana, generates $100 million in sales at above-industry-average profits despite the fact that its sales reps are outnumbered by those of its competitors—G. E. Plastics ($2 billion in plastics), DuPont ($3 billion in plastics), and Monsanto ($1 billion in plastics). Akzo's sales growth has averaged 14 percent per year since 1987 in an industry that is growing at only 6 percent per year. It achieves this growth and share by focusing on small-volume but high-profit niches for conductive plastics for electronics, internally lubricated plastics (used in self-lubricating gears and bearings for copiers, computers, and office equipment), ultra-high-impact-resistant plastics (used in car dashboards and on car mirrors), and flame retardant plastics (used in household appliances). Akzo re-educated its sales reps, who had to be taught that selling high-volume truckloads of low-margin materials was not Akzo's specialty. Akzo trained its reps to become market development specialists who work in tandem with marketers and Akzo's product design engineers to ferret out high-profit plastics applications in selected end-user segments.

Greater sales productivity through market focus often dictates that a company's sales reps learn new skills. Air Products and Chemicals, Inc., faced this challenge when its reps moved from selling bulk commodity-type chemicals to specialties. Bulk chemical customers—a small number of big accounts which order infrequently—dictate service and selling in large order lot sizes. Specialty chemical users, on the other hand, want frequent shipments in small quantities, and they are extremely demanding about just-in-time order turnaround. Air Products and Chemicals not only had to re-direct its reps to provide new services, it had to invest in a new on-line order and credit system to facilitate the reps' demands to have information always available on where small customers' orders were in the supply fulfilment cycle.

Boosting sales productivity also requires that a business encourage and support its reps in turning first-time customers into repeat or lifetime buyers. Even a small change in customer retention can have a big effect on an industry's profitability. For example, in the insurance brokerage business, retaining 90 percent of yearly customers may enable a brokerage to break even; retaining 95–97 percent can mean generating excellent profits. This orientation is the reason so many auto manufacturers try to keep their car buyers coming back for future auto purchases.

Boosting Productivity in Distribution

Distribution, like sales, can represent a fertile area for productivity gains. Productive marketing channel selection can boost sales. The initial marketers of digital wristwatches learned this lesson. Initially they tried to sell their digital watches through traditional jewellers' stores. These stores had a vested interest in selling what they stocked—the more traditional chronolog watches—so the digital watch producers couldn't get store listings. When they eventually tried nontraditional channels such as drug and hardware stores they had great success. They then moved their watches into more mainstream mass merchandising stores. Digital watches became such a big hit in a few short years that the original distribution channel chosen—independent jewellers—had to go back to digital watch producers cap in hand and seek to get the product for their display cases.

Physical distribution productivity can have tremendous payoffs. Both Levi Strauss and Toyota have shortened distribution time by linking themselves to their retailers (in Levi's case) or their dealers (in Toyota's case) by computer. Information on daily sales is transmitted on-line to Levi or Toyota. This information allows each company to detect buying patterns immediately, shift production to reflect such patterns, and thus reduce unwanted inventory and its assorted costs. Data from the channel drives production forecasts and replenishment decisions.

More just-in-time buying pattern information also assists in both scheduling factory machinery and determining raw material delivery requirements. Productivity is boosted through improved capacity utilization and more accurate and exacting raw material procurement. All parts of the process flow materials better, eliminating surpluses and holding times. Minimizing inventories reduces the costs associated with such inventories, such as material handling costs, insurance costs, shrinkage, spoilage or breakage costs, obsolescence costs, financing costs, downtime costs (idle time caused by, for example, the delivery of the wrong raw materials at a machine center), labor costs, and fuel costs (if finished goods or work in process have to travel long distances in the warehouse or factory *unnecessarily*). Computer linkages used to boost distribution productivity can often also be used to exchange invoices and purchase orders and release date information between suppliers and customers, further cutting order processing, credit checking, and delayed- or lost-order expediting costs.

Productivity in Advertising and Sales Promotion

Spending on advertising and sales promotion continues unabated. In 1989, U.S.-based media advertising totalled $70.7 billion, while sales promotion topped $135 billion! Each of these totals has doubled since 1982. (See Figure 1-3 for these spending totals.) Clearly marketing productivity demands that advertising and sales promotion spending be well thought out to avoid waste from target decisions, creative cost decisions, and media buying decisions. In fact, planning for ads and promotions today more and more resembles the construction of an intricate mosaic. Decisions must be taken on a vast array of possible promotion, advertising, and business merchandising combinations. A business may have to decide whether to use price-offs, event marketing, third-party endorsements, point-of-sale displays, or a blend of approaches.

The productivity rule most important for targeting messages

Figure 1-3. U.S. advertising and promotion spending in 1989 ($ in billions).

		$ Spent	%
Advertising	**TV**	$ 25.4	36%
	Radio	7.9	11
	Business Press	2.7	4
	Consumer Print	6.4	9
	Newspapers	26.8	38
	Other, Including Outdoor	1.5	2
	Total	$ 70.7	100%
Sales Promotion	**Direct Mail**	$ 21.9	16%
	Point of Purchase	18.4	14
	Premiums/Incentives	17.8	13
	Meetings/Conventions	37.6	28
	Trade Shows	8.8	6
	Promotional Advertising	11.3	8
	Print/AV	13.1	10
	Coupon Redemption	6.3	5
	Total	$135.2	100%

Source: Figures adapted from several tables in Ross Bowman, "Sales Promotion," *Marketing and Media Decisions* Magazine (July 1990), p. 21.

successfully is: The more precise the targeting, the less wasteful the spending. If a company can target its intended audience precisely, it then has the best chance of finding a medium that delivers that desired audience. For example, companies targeting teenagers, such as Burger King, Frito-Lay, M&M/Mars, and Nike, use Whittle Communications Channel One, a television medium (delivered via satellite) that reaches inside 4,000 of the nation's high schools to provide programming. Other advertisers seeking to sell cosmetics, clothes, and health and beauty products to teens can reach them by MTV, the music video television channel. Such precise targeting doesn't waste ad dollars since few nontargeted viewers are watching. A cross-promotion on a shared cost basis between companies that target identical customers is an excellent productivity idea. Lego Systems and Kellogg undertook such a venture when Kellogg put coupons for Lego inside and ads on the outside of boxes of Kellogg's Fruit Loops; each company was targeting kids two to five years old.

Evian Waters of France, a bottled water supplier, is an excellent example of a company that targets its prospective drinkers very productively. Having determined that a high percentage of its drinkers are tennis players, Evian sponsors men's tennis tour events; it provides Evian coolers to tournaments for the players' refreshment (and Evian TV exposure); it runs ads in the tennis programs sold to the public; it sells Evian to the spectators at tennis tournament concessions; and it gives tennis tournament tickets to its local distributors. In 1987, the cost of all these promotions was only $30,000 for six major tennis events. The campaign was so successful that Evian in 1988 expanded the program to cover seventeen tournaments, including the U.S. Tennis Open. The success of Evian's promotional efforts has boosted sales to over $60 million in 1989.

The United Dairy Association has similarly boosted sales of dairy products by judicious targeting of buyers. It uses point-of-purchase advertising in supermarkets and convenience stores instead of mass media electronic or print ads. These efforts have proven productive in triggering impulse sales of a variety of dairy products, from cheese to yogurt.

Creative Costs

Getting leverage from creative advertising costs often requires the creation of a message or campaign for which the same creative can be reproduced in a variety of formats. For example, ads that are used for print publications and that can be reworked with little additional expense for point-of-sale, catalog covers, sales handouts for sales calls, and calendars for distributors' offices or showrooms provide for a much stronger payoff than single-use ads.

Sharing creative materials with a business's dealers or retailers in cooperative advertising plans also ensures that higher productivity comes from the creative development by the company's ad agency. For instance, Quaker State Corporation buys sixty-second radio spots in a variety of local markets across the United States. It uses the first thirty seconds for its branded ads and the remaining thirty seconds for its local retailers' ads, which are tied to a local special promotion of Quaker State products. Local retailers in essence piggyback on Quaker State's creative lead-in.

One interesting productivity initiative by advertisers is the resurrection of old familiar campaign slogans or symbols. RCA is resurrecting Nipper the dog. Pillsbury its Poppin' Fresh Dough-boy, and Shell Oil its Shell "Answer Man" (a character it featured between 1976 and 1982). Even Procter & Gamble is bringing back the Mariner Man who used to be featured in Old Spice TV commercials—albeit with a more upscale "thirtysomething" image. Consumer research demonstrates that some of these symbols and characters are still great for attracting viewer attention; for instance, Shell's Answer Man is now used to demonstrate Shell's concern for customer satisfaction. An interesting spin-off of this resurrection tactic for "old" creative is to alter the original in a novel way. Timex, for example, is bringing back its slogan, "Takes a licking but keeps on ticking," by applying the slogan to people who have survived despite adversity. The ads feature noncelebrities who have confronted some incredible mishap or bad luck to survive unharmed and full of life. They include people struck by lightning, attacked by wild boars, or sucked into water-intake systems or who have fallen eighty-five feet straight down from a cliff. For thirteen years, Old Milwaukee told beer drinkers "It doesn't get any better than this" by picturing buddies out trout fishing together. A new campaign claims the old ads were wrong; it *does* get better. The new commercial picks up where the old one left off, but adds a few new wrinkles to the composite. These include a live band on the beach, lobsters falling from planes, those old buddies finding softball-sized gold nuggets in a stream, and a Swedish bikini team parachuting into the composite. Obviously, gaining attention, awareness, and sales from creative concepts paid for long ago is an ideal productivity tactic.

Media Buying

Another productivity measure in advertising involves buying media wisely. This may mean spending on regional instead of national promotions because the regional media can deliver more customized messages. For instance, Andrew Jergens Company, which makes hand lotions, chooses local media and customizes hand lotion messages according to the local market it wishes to reach. In Denver, its ads tie into skiing (hand cream for cold, chapped hands), while in Milwaukee, Jergens' ads and promotions are tied to bowling (Jergens' lotions "smooth the rough spots in a bowler's game"). The more localized the media, the more customized a promotion can be. For example, in a local promotion in Chicago, McDonald's drops its prices for a Quarter Pounder With Cheese whenever the Chicago Bears football team wins.

As large magazine publishing groups begin to dominate the ownership of multiple magazines, media buying deals become increasingly possible for advertisers. Such deals can allow an advertiser to buy multiple magazine placements for a lower price than the per page insertion costs of purchasing each magazine alone. Some advertisers have cut their media costs by inserting their commercials onto videotaped hit movies rented at video shops. Nestlé has done this and has had much success, with its ads being seen by thousands of movie renters.

Of course, the ultimate in advertising productivity is to keep sales high with little or no advertising at all. This has been the very successful formula of wholesale clubs such as the Price Club, a fifty-outlet $5 billion (in sales) chain. Wholesale clubs keep their prices very low by minimizing any advertising to attract shoppers. Instead, they develop a membership that is entitled to cash in on the wholesale club's rock-bottom price offerings on brand-name merchandise. The presence of a select membership customer base eliminates the need for extensive advertising, which in turn helps wholesale clubs keep their operating costs lower than those of competitive retailers. Typical members are small-business owners, professionals, and self-employed work-at-home types. These clubs have been so successful that combined volume from all U.S. wholesale clubs exceeded $17.5 billion in 1989, up from $7 billion in 1986 and almost nothing in the early 1980s.

Other Sales Promotion Productivity Techniques

Sales promotion spending productivity ideas abound. They vary from finding lower-cost methods of couponing products (in-store dispensers, for instance) and providing free samples (perhaps by distribution to passengers on airline flights) to boosting responses from direct mail programs (such as by using cross promotion, shared spending ideas, with other companies). One example of a productive promotion is that used by Campbell Soup, Pepperidge Farm Desserts, and V-8 Juice, all of which boosted their coupon redemption rates from three to four percent (average for these products) to eight percent by dispensing their coupons in a local market via automated teller machines in Memphis, Nashville, and Knoxville, Tennessee. (The automated teller machines were owned by a local promotion partner, the National Bank of Commerce.)

Productive sales promotion ideas can often be combined. For example, Sears sells the McKids clothing line, which feature McDonald's licensed characters. McDonald's gains advertising exposure plus licensing fees while Sears gains incremental sales. Sears took the idea one step further, however, by issuing meal coupons redeemable at McDonald's, the redemption value of which was based upon the amount of a Sears customer's purchases of McKids clothing.

Many of the techniques of sales promotion (direct mail, leads generated, coupons redeemed, samples handed out or delivered) are directly measurable. The effectiveness of efforts to boost productivity can often be precisely gauged. This is not the case with advertising spending changes, where results that flow from productivity initiatives can be measured on the cost side (did the ads cost more, the same, or less?) but are often difficult, if not impossible, to measure on the revenue side.

Determining the effect of ad spending changes on revenues can prove difficult. That is why so much attention is paid to trying to measure changes in awareness, purchase intentions, recall, or some other measure less direct than sales generated by changes in advertising.

Productivity in Other Marketing Tactical Areas

While the major tactical spending areas of marketing are product line management, selling, distribution, and advertising and promotion, there are other tactical areas where productive spending can boost a company's performance.

Packaging

Companies may decide to repackage their products in an effort to cut waste, enhance reusability of containers, provide for a more environmentally friendly package that is easier and less harmful to dispose of, or give the package an alternate use beyond its primary use (for example, peanut butter in glasses). When Procter & Gamble redesigned its package for secret brand deodorant, it was able to pack thirty-six bottles to a shipping carton, instead of twenty-four, as in the past. The change cut its packaging costs, shipping costs (it shipped less air), and storage costs, *and* it cut its retail customers' handling costs.

Repackaging can even wake up sales of an older product. For example, most competitors of industrial cleaning chemicals ship to customers in 55-gallon drums, which customers have to handle, store, and clean for re-use. In California, Technology Chemical provides its customers with large tanks, which it installs on their site for free. It then delivers product in bulk and refills the tank on site, which saves its customers time and money otherwise spent handling drums. Technology Chemical's sales of these cleaning chemicals have grown rapidly, even though these are very mature products.

Market Research

Market research costs can often be made more productive with creativity. Trade shows can be an excellent way to distribute research questionnaires or discuss new products in person with prospective customers. Omnibus market research surveys lower the costs of research, since these multi-client participation studies allow a company to insert questions for much less money than a separate stand-alone survey would cost.

Oil companies often run "lucky-draw" contests at their new service stations. Customers fill out cards calling for their names and addresses to win the prize; in plotting the addresses on a map, the oil company can determine the exact size of the trading area that the station is drawing its customers from—inexpensive but valuable market research—all for the cost of a small prize giveaway (such as a clock radio). With this market research the oil company knows where to distribute local coupons for its car wash, mechanical repair specials, or special sale flyers for tires or batteries.

Public Relations

Making public relations spending more productive often means finding ways to get public exposure for your products at low or minimal cost. Amana, Turtle Wax, and Jolly Time popcorn became well-known household brands in the United States by buying inexpensive ten-second television spots on television game shows, which gave away their products as prizes.

The British seem to have a particular flair for low-cost, high-exposure publicity. Nevica, Ltd., is a London-based skiwear manufacturer that has grown into a $60-million-a-year brand selling in the United Kingdom, Australia, New Zealand, Europe, and even in the heart of Colorado. Nevica didn't advertise its flashy neon ski designs. Instead it offered the world's top thirty ski magazine photographers free clothes and a small fee if they would put Nevica skiwear on models used to advertise *other* ski attractions or products. As a result, Nevica's clothes started turning up in all sorts of ads for ski resorts, ski boots, skis, bindings, and even feature stories on skiing techniques and exotic locations.

In one clever gimmick, a new British science fiction and horror magazine's management wondered how to sell out its first issue. They came up with the idea of surveying men and women to determine what percentage would be more frightened by Freddy, the lead psychopath of *Nightmare on Elm Street*, than by being marooned on an island alone with Margaret Thatcher. Since 36 percent of men said the Margaret Thatcher scenario scared them more (only 20 percent of women felt this way), predictably the British papers and television stations picked up this amusing tidbit for news broadcasts. The first issue of *Dark Side* sold out completely on British newsstands.

Distributor Incentives

Providing incentives to distributors is a typical marketing expense for many companies that sell their products through middlemen. What is difficult is finding a way to do this productively, rather than merely launching free-goods promotions or off-invoice deals, which in effect erode average selling prices.

American Olean Tile Company of Lansdale, Pennsylvania, boosted sales of its ceramic floor tile and colored grouts by 82 percent over the previous year by awarding merchandise prizes to its distributor's reps for selling new contractor accounts. Distributor reps earned fifty points for every thousand square feet of tile sold to new accounts. Low-end merchandise prizes such as electronic typewriters, cordless phones, or food processors were valued at 300 to 500 points; bigger prizes, such as rolltop desks, video cameras, or personal computers, cost a distributor rep 1,000 points or more. More than 264 distributor reps earned prizes and close to 250 new contractor or dealer accounts were opened. Clearly, the prizes were self-liquidating, since incremental profits on the new business generated more than covered the $150,000 cost of the nationwide incentive program.

Pricing Plan Productivity

Gaining productivity improvement from pricing plans calls for a solid understanding of how high the company can price its products before it reaches the upper limit of price sensitivity with its customers and risks losing business. This fact in turn often dictates that the company segment its customers into groups by price bracket, so that it avoids using an average pricing approach in which it tries to make one price list suit all customer segments. Such a pricing system results in overcharging very price-sensitive customers and leaving money on the table with less price-sensitive buyers.

For instance, a specialty glass manufacturer boosted its volume and profits by moving from a single price list to setting prices by market. Its glass was sold to two distinct sets of customers—original equipment manufacturers and buyers of replacement glass. While original equipment manufacturers' customers were very price-sensitive, replacement glass buyers were not; they wanted ready availability and name-brand quality assurance. The manufacturer began to sell to original equipment manufacturers in large lots at lower prices and to replacement buyers at higher prices through distributors who could meet their needs for just-in-time availability. General Electric keeps average pricing high on its appliances by selling GE branded appliances at higher prices than its own Hotpoint brand, which is targeted at the more price-sensitive end of the market. Branding by price position is a common variant used in pushing for maximum price.

Optimizing Leverage of Intangible Assets

As Figure 1-1 illustrates, a company has both tangible "real" assets and intangible assets. In this chapter, I have given numerous examples of ways to boost productivity from selling, marketing, and distribution spending and in turn to leverage the hard assets that underlie these—inventories, sales locations, warehousing systems, and so on. In addition, this chapter has also delineated how to exploit patents, to maximize customer retention, and to boost the productivity of distribution channels.

Of all intangible assets, brand names are perhaps the most valuable, because they often transcend the physical properties of a product in the minds of customers, as well as providing for very long revenue streams when managed wisely.

Consider the case of Geritol, a brand that languished until very recently because its image as a geriatric product hurt it at a time when active and fit consumers age 50 and over don't think of themselves as old. Geritol has been rebranded as Geritol Extend and has been repositioned as a multi-vitamin, just perfect for active, vital over-50 consumers. Backed by promotions such as Big Band Bash sponsorships (including swing dance competitions) and walking rallies for seniors, Geritol Extend has bounced back from negative sales growth to double digit (19 percent) annual sales gains. The ability to tap into Geritol's strong name recognition and to alter basic brand beliefs demonstrate vividly the latent leveraging power of intangible assets such as brands.

Notes

1. Gretchen Morgenson, "The Buy-Out That Saved Safeway," *Forbes* (November 12, 1990), p. 92.
2. Allan J. Magrath, *Market Smarts: Proven Strategies to Outfox and Outflank Your Competition* (New York: John Wiley & Sons, 1988), pp. 7–23.
3. Steve Weiner, "Don't Merge, Joint Venture," *Forbes* (November 12, 1990), p. 39.
4. David Woodruff, "Has Dow Chemical Found the Right Formula?" *Business Week* (August 7, 1990), p. 62.
5. Walter G. Schmid, "Heinz Covers the Globe," *Journal of Business Strategy* (March–April 1989), p. 20.
6. Michael D'Amato and Jeremy Silverman, "How to Make Money in a Dull Business," *Across the Board* (December 1990), p. 59.
7. "Defy the Odds," *Success* (November 1989), p. 18.
8. "Hotel Industry Faces Glut and Large Deficits," *The Wall Street Journal* (November 21, 1990), pp. A1, A7.
9. "Reducing the Bile Factor at Heinz," *Fortune* (April 9, 1990), p. 42.
10. Monica Roman, "How DuPont Keeps 'em Coming Back for More," *Business Week* (August 20, 1990), p. 68.
11. "Valley of the Dolls," *The Economist* (December 16, 1989), p. 66. Also see Gretchen Morgenson, "Barbie Does Budapest," *Forbes* (January 7, 1991), pp. 66–69.
12. "Companies to Watch," *Fortune* (September 10, 1990), p. 95.
13. Alyssa Lappen, "Defying the Law of Gravity," *Forbes* (April 3, 1989), p. 77.
14. Allan J. Magrath, *The Revolution in Sales and Marketing,* (New York: AMACOM Books, 1990), pp. 33–34.
15. William A. O'Connell, "A Ten Year Report on Sales Productivity," *Sales & Marketing Management* (December 1988), p. 33.
16. Sandra Pesmen, "Taking off the Gloves in Hard Times," *Business Marketing* (January 1991), p. 12.
17. See Richard J. Schonberger, *Building a Chain of Customers* (New York: The Free Press, 1990) for a fuller exploration of the benefits in productivity from teamwork among sales, the factory, and the technical part of the organization.

2

Marketing Innovation and Competitive Advantage

Businessmen love numbers. Numbers make them feel secure. . . .
As they grow, corporations tend to lose this feel for the market
. . . they start to manage by numbers. Managers begin to worry
about the efficiencies of mass production and less about the needs
of the market. Managers must maintain their intuitive feel for
market trends and attitudes. They should look at the numbers,
but they shouldn't be ruled by them.

Regis McKenna
The Regis Touch

Chief executives and senior management of American companies are greatly concerned about the innovativeness of their marketing organizations. In one major survey of eighteen of the leading package goods companies in the United States, McKinsey and Company[1] found that 92 percent of their senior executives were dissatisfied with the level of marketing innovativeness in their marketing programs and strategies and within their marketing ranks.

This lack of innovativeness can cripple an organization, since the pace of change is quickening in every aspect of business. Industries, products, customers, competitors, and distribution channels are changing, and companies that do not or cannot innovatively adapt or react to change will pay a heavy price for keeping the blinders on. U.S. auto companies ignored, and Japanese car makers listened to, growing demands for small cars. As a result, the Japanese stole market share from their rivals. Ten years ago the computer software industry included hundreds of companies; today there are thousands. In the mid-1960s six important U.S. industries—autos, steel, consumer electronics (televisions, stereos, VCRs), calculators, machine tools, and textiles—faced the loss of less than 10 percent of their market to imported competition. By 1981 the picture had changed dramatically. The United States imported 26 percent of its cars, almost 20 percent of its steel, 60 percent of its consumer electronics, over 40 percent of its calculators, more than half of all its machine tools, and 35 percent of its textiles. Why? Because companies in these industries did not innovate, so their customers left them in droves.

Innovation Is a Disruptive Force

As companies grow, they seek operating efficiency in order to drive costs lower and gain market share. The emphasis on innovation in marketing, so dominant when the business was developing its new products, often shifts to focus on innovation in manufacturing processes. Companies invest in special-purpose machinery to produce new products in repetitive, predictable ways. Management often worries more about manufacturing and servicing demand and less about serving any new needs that may still exist unfilled in the market. IBM focussed so much on producing PCs that it missed the laptop market needs of its customers.

Mass production mindsets inhibit innovation and change because the organizational processes that foster efficiency are often diametrically opposed to those that foster innovation. Efficiency calls for coordination, streamlining, leveraging of assets and business systems, and eliminating slack wherever feasible. Innovation, on the other hand, is often a messy, wasteful process that flourishes in an organizational climate of experimentation, trial and error, false starts, and high information exchange. It requires ample available resources to thrive. Teamwork and small-team competition are often present in innovative organizations. Sharp Electronics has used close to 150 teams to develop new products from an LCD projection television to the Electronic

Organizer. Bureaucracy and "bigness" can often freeze out innovation as employees become wedded to certain ideas, products, and technologies, and a "rule by numbers" mentality takes over. New markets, new products, or new ideas that do not have a statistically-based projection to substantiate them don't get management support.

Yet new markets and emerging markets often defy projections. Customer surveys may not even turn up a sufficient number of customers to justify a new product innovation. For example, in 1976 very few people considered themselves in need of a personal computer; yet today, hundreds of thousands of such machines are sold each month.

Creativity is often the key to new markets. Companies must innovate through market creation rather than extrapolating from the past or following some existing industry standard. Apple Computer didn't clone the IBM personal computer's architecture or operating systems; its engineers created a unique machine— the Macintosh. 3M had no idea when they invented Scotch brand tape that a market could be developed for its more than 400 separate tape constructions. If 3M had stopped innovating and had instead concentrated on the status quo versus growth and creativity, it would be a much smaller, less vital corporation. The world would also be without some basic products that 3M invented, such as videotape. When Yamaha applied digital sound technology to pianos and changed their form, they created electronic compact keyboards. Customer research wouldn't have led them to this new product; new piano shapes or functions just weren't thought about.

To encourage innovation in marketing, organizations need to accept and deal with uncertainty. Market "need substantiation" cannot always be reduced to a science. Marketers who wish to stress innovativeness and adaptation to change need to stop trying to always predict the unpredictable.

Many successful businesses have been created despite a lack of hard data to document a demand for their product or service. For example, digital readout devices, which have been successful in the marketplace, were not demanded by a ready market; companies invented the technology and then identified possible customer applications for it. Marketers must also learn not to rest on past successes. Today's popular product may be tomorrow's trivia question. Being conservative is like playing not to lose (vs. innovating continually and playing to win). Nike and Reebok continually "mess with their success" by inventing new sports shoes. Understanding a market for mature products is akin to understanding a game such as handball, in which the market environment is confined and the players (competitors) limited. Playing the "new market game," however, is more analogous to playing soccer—the field is wide open, and there are lots of players, lots of options, and many possibilities.

The Six Pathways Leading to Innovation

Since the capacity to innovate is critical to outpacing competitors in a dynamic environment, it is imperative that each business understand the many pathways it can follow to boost innovation. There are at least six different innovation pathways worthy of understanding and knowledge (see Figure 2-1).

1. *Innovation based on core technologies.* Exploitation spins off new different and disparate products. This sort of innovative behavior is characteristic of companies such as Canon, NEC, Casio, Honda, 3M, and Sony. A poll of Japanese executives conducted by Nippon Hoso Kyokai, a market research firm, found an overwhelmingly belief that the key to Japan's growth in the 1990s would derive from innovations resulting from techno-logical capabilities.

2. *Innovation based on a unique remix of common operating ele-ments.* Retailers and service businesses such as The Gap, The Limited, Nordstrom, The Body Shop, Uniforce Temporary Person-nel, Toys "R" Us, Home Depot, and American Express pursue this pathway. They believe that what the business does or sells is less the source of its innovation than the manner in which it does it. So while The Gap's clothing is not impressively unique, its method of merchandising and presenting these fashions is.

3. *Innovation that satisfies unmet customer needs.* These needs may relate to new product uses, new product designs with

Figure 2-1. Six pathways to innovation.

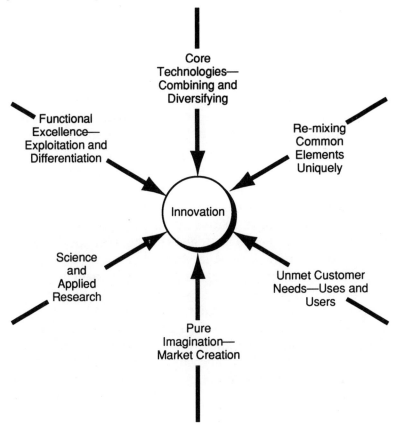

appeal, or the innovative tapping of new groups of product users. Companies particularly astute at using this pathway include Procter & Gamble, Black & Decker, Nike, Rubbermaid, and entrepreneurs such as Ben and Jerry's Gourmet Ice Cream.

4. *Innovation created from pure imagination.* Often this type of innovative marketing goes on in creative businesses such as publishing, film production, television, and the arts. Notable company examples include Norman Lear's Act III Communications (producers of *Maude* and *All in The Family*), Henson Associates, Hanna Barbera (cartoon shows), Andrew Lloyd Webber Productions, and the Walt Disney Company. In fact, Disney as a

company has given the lexicon of marketing a whole new term—
"imagineering"—that describes its formula for business innovativeness.

5. *Innovation based on scientific research.* Companies pursuing
this axis of innovation include pharmaceutical companies such as
Merck and Glaxo, diversified companies such as DuPont and
Corning, and biotech companies such as Genentech. Innovation
is synonymous in many of these businesses with scientific discoveries or applied laboratory research and development.

6. *Innovation based on functional excellence.* Companies following this path focus on specific functions in their operations and
then leverage these functions to outdo competitors and to innovate through the use of specialized functional expertise. Porsche,
for instance, has grown thanks to its engineering excellence,
Frito-Lay to its excellence in logistics, the Four Seasons hotel
chain to excellence in personalized guest services, Dow Jones to
its expertise in information system services management, Wrigley's Gum to its merchandising excellence, and L. L. Bean to its
expertise in mail-order direct marketing. In effect, such companies hone in on functions that can provide them with a leg up
on their rivals, and then they proceed to out-innovate these
rivals over time along this innovation axis. Some management
experts have termed these corporate functional skills "core com-
petencies."

Innovation Spun From Core Technologies

A number of companies have prospered by utilizing their technological expertise in creative ways. For example, Honda's core
technologies involve engineering small motors and power trains.
It has exploited these technologies in motorcycles, automobiles,
lawn mowers, generators, and a myriad of other products. Its
core technologies are the springboard for its new products and
market entries.

Canon's core technologies are in fine optics, precision mechanics, and microelectronic componentry. As a result of its
technologies, it has innovated in cameras, copiers, facsimile
equipment, calculators, laser printers, and still-video cameras.

Each product represents some combination of its technologies in design, features, and functions. Cameras, for example, require optics, as do copiers. Microelectronics are present in fax machines, copiers, autofocus cameras, and laser printers.

By combining and recombining such technologies, innovation can create product families. Canon, for example, began by manufacturing simple cameras, then moved into autofocus cameras and still-video cameras. Similarly, from plain paper copiers Canon moved on to color copiers, color laser copiers, and battery-powered plain paper copiers. Technological combinations of diverse technologies often broaden product offerings.

3M's technologies in precision coating, adhesives, flexible backings and substrates, and various films has generated thousands of products, from coated abrasives to tapes, videocassettes, diskettes, photographic film, Post-it notes, fastening systems, graphic arts films, surgical incise drapes, and reflective sheeting for road signs. Companies whose innovation pathway involves exploiting diverse technologies constantly tinker and refine each technology as well as combine them with others. For instance, 3M's coating technology in tapes has been exploited for hundreds of different sorts of tape, including tapes for office use, medical use, veterinarian use, automotive use (paint masking, tape to hold on car moldings or nameplates), electrical use, packaging use, aerospace use (ultra-high bonding tapes), highway use (center lane marking tapes), and even for fastening disposable diapers. Such technology exploitation broadens marketing's customer base; if the product use becomes widespread across markets, global geographic spread becomes possible.

Innovation Spun From Core Technologies: The Case of Sony Corporation

Sony Corporation is an example of a company that has spun innovation after innovation from its core know-how in audio and video technology. (Innovations derived from its core technologies in audio and video electronics are listed in Figure 2-2.) Founded in 1946 in war-ravaged Tokyo, the company continues to market new products that have not only given it more than $17 billion in sales worldwide but have changed the life-style of a generation,

Figure 2-2. Sony Corporation: products derived from core technologies.

Core Technologies	Starter Products (1940s–1950s)	Later Products (1960s, 1970s, 1980s)
Audio	Tape Recorders	Walkman
	Microphones	Compact Disc
		Compact Disc Players
		Portable Compact Disc Players
	Audio Cassettes	Digital Audio Tape
		Digital Audio Tape Players
		Portable Digital Audio Tape Players
		Digital Audio Tape Players for Cars
		"My First Sony" for Children
Video	Televisions/Monitors	VCR (Betamax)
	Television Cameras	Trinitron TV
	Television Editors	High-Definition TV
		Watchman
		Videotape
		Camcorders (hand-held video cameras)
		35mm filmless camera ("Mavica")
		Electronic Sketch Pads (draws pictures on TV, replays on VCR)
		Workstations for Offices

with products such as the Sony Walkman. Sony's research and development efforts consume 6–8 percent of its sales yearly, considerably more than the 5 percent or less spent by rivals Pioneer, JVC, and AIWA.

A great number of Sony's products are "firsts"—new-to-the-world innovations. For instance, Sony beat its archrivals Technics and JVC in coming out with the first portable digital audio tape player and the first digital audio tape player for cars, announced in September 1990. Sony's Walkman, introduced in 1979, has sold more than 50 million units since its debut, and Sony continues to manufacture one million Walkmans a month. Sony's expertise in audio and video tapes and discs has also led it into new fields, such as data cartridges, that utilize its magnetic media manufacturing skills.

To ensure that all of Sony's research and development effort and investments in new products pay off, Sony has sought stronger control of its business. For example, its purchase of CBS Records for $2.2 billion in January 1988 gives it assurance that its compact discs will be used as the medium of choice by CBS recording artists and possibly other engineers. Its acquisition of Columbia Pictures for $3.4 billion in November 1989 similarly provides assurance that Sony's videotape will be used to duplicate Columbia's library of 2,700 movies, which will then be broadcast on Sony's high-definition televisions using its proprietary 8mm film format.

Companies such as Sony that innovate from core technologies frequently find that the approach can be a hit-or-miss proposition. Sony has had its share of failures, including a dedicated word processor launched in the early 1980s for industrial customers that was surpassed in power and flexibility by the personal computer; its Betamax video recorder, which in the late 1970s was surpassed by the less costly VHS format; and its instant photo camera which in the 1950s worked only with black-and-white film and was surpassed by Polaroid's color models.

Sony is attempting to pursue its pathway toward innovation by diversifying its core technologies. It is introducing workstations for industrial use and developing personal computers that can read data written by hand (which could open up a huge new market for personal computer use among truck drivers, rack jobbers, and others who have personal computer applications but no way to type in their inputs).

Sony has also been relentless in exploiting its new products to the fullest. For example, its Walkman comes in endless variations, including a waterproof sports models, a childproof version[2] for four- to twelve-year-olds, and a Watchman.

In addition to diversifying its technologies, Sony is spreading its research and development centers around the world, modelling itself after IBM (which has twenty centers in fourteen different countries). Since 1988 Sony has established two new centers, one in Stuttgart, Germany, and one in Basingstoke, United Kingdom. In 1990, these centers employed 200 scientists, compared with only fifty, two years earlier. Sony appears to be decentralizing research and development efforts so that each of its key regional companies—Sony of America, Sony Europe, Sony Asia, and Sony Japan—is encouraged to design, produce, and market its own innovative product lines. Thus, the "My First Sony" line of kids' products was developed by Sony Corporation of America.

Sony is hopeful that its diversification into regional units will boost its innovativeness and smooth its profits, which have been erratic in the past. For instance, Sony made 132.7 billion yen profit in 1981; by 1983 its profit dropped to only 51.4 billion yen.

Innovation by exploiting core technologies can be a very powerful way to grow if two conditions are met: Research and development must be steady and high (which is not always possible if debt costs are overly high), and the quality of research and development management must be excellent to ensure that a healthy *yield* of new products is always forthcoming. Sony's use of a high proportion of debt to equity to buy a movie studio and a record company may create problems in funding steady, sustained research and development at levels higher than those of its major rivals. However, Sony is the envy of many companies for its excellent batting average in new product creation.

Innovation From Remixing Common Elements Uniquely

While invention can be a powerful way to propel a business's growth, as the Sony example demonstrates, some companies' innovation strategy is more basic, involving reshuffling elements that are often common to its competitors but doing it in a way that makes the company stand out or attract a new customer base. Outstanding retailers provide excellent illustrations of this type of innovation.

Almost any major retailer shares in common with others identical strategy elements—its inventory levels and assortments, its strategy on store size and locations, its pricing posture, its staffing, its hours of operation, its store displays and decor, and its credit policies. Innovation therefore comes from creatively remixing all or some of these to provide uniqueness.

Montgomery Ward is pursuing this axis of innovation, re-making itself from a national chain department store into a retailer housing six distinct specialty stores under its roof. In effect, it is no longer presenting itself as a full assortment retailer. It has remixed its merchandise assortments and store design elements (colors, signing, and layout) and offers the consumer specialized retail stores conveniently inside four walls—Electric Avenue, which sells home electronics; The Apparel Store (men's, women's and children's clothes); Gold and Gems, a jewelry specialist; Auto Express (auto parts); Kids Store; and Home Ideas, which specialties in home textiles and accessories. None of the remixed elements are foreign to its rivals, but the unique way in which Montgomery Ward has positioned and implemented the remixing is the genesis of its marketing innovation.

Wal-Mart is innovatively different from Kmart or Target not in the merchandise it sells but in its ability to offer the best price-value trade-off to customers in presenting the merchandise for sale. Because of its excellence, Wal-Mart now exceeds Sears in sales, making it the largest retailer in the United States (1990 sales were $32.6 billion versus Sears at $31.9 billion).

Home Depot's lumber and do-it-yourself offerings do not set it apart from other chains. What Home Depot does is outservice its rivals by using much more knowledgeable in-store staff who can talk intelligently about do-it-yourself projects. Most are for-mer tradespeople, such as plumbers, electricians, or carpenters. Home Depot has taken one key element of its retailing mix, namely staffing, and altered it in a way competitors haven't matched. While the element it has changed is not new, the way it has transformed it *is* new. It has freshened its service dimension innovatively.

Other stores select other aspects of the retailing mix to focus their creative energies on. For example, The Gap uses themed promotions for its clothing four times a year to set itself apart from other apparel retailers. Nieman-Marcus uses its choice of inventory to be unique, as do Crate & Barrel and Saks Fifth

Avenue. The Limited uses a combination of unique merchandise and unique decor/store displays to set itself apart innovatively.

In manufacturing, differentiating the physical product with features is at best quite short-lived. Competitors often quickly figure out what you did and how to match what was done. It is often better to take a common strategy element and innovate with it. Braun, a Gillette subsidiary, has done this for many years using innovative product design. Its shavers, hair care products, and household appliances (such as coffee makers and clocks) are very distinctive in visual and tactile appeal, materials used, and compactness. For instance, its KF40 coffee maker, launched in 1984, sold 400,000 units its first year and won numerous design awards in Europe. Today Braun sells 2.5 million units a year of this uniquely designed coffee maker. While all of its rivals use design as a tool in their marketing mix, nobody uses it as skillfully as Braun in the product categories in which it competes. It has remixed a very standard differentiating marketing element with outstanding innovation.[3]

Colgate-Palmolive markets Science Diet and Prescription Diet brand pet foods through its Hill's Pet Products subsidiary. But unlike most companies that sell pet foods in supermarkets, Colgate sells its product at 20,000 U.S. veterinarians' offices and pet stores. It has remixed a common strategy element—distribution channel selection—in a unique way. The result? Its pet foods sell for an average of $2 per can compared to a typical supermarket price of sixty-nine cents a can for its competitors. Hill's sells $1 billion a year worth of pet food and is responsible for 25 percent of Colgate's total corporate profits.

Innovation in a service business can also be accomplished by remixing common strategy elements. Uniforce Temporary Personnel[4] has grown from a $43 million company offering temporary personnel to clients through thirty franchises in 1984 to a $110 million outfit selling at 110 offices. It achieved this growth using many standard franchiser services, such as training and administrative services (managing franchisees' insurance, taxes, and payroll), but also by innovating in the area of cash flow assistance to franchisees. While most local temp services pay their employees weekly and have to wait four to six weeks to be paid by their clients, Uniforce pays franchisee temps from its central funds, relieving franchisees of having to wait for their money with a starved cash flow. Uniforce has found that when franchisees worry less about cash flow, they can spend more time learning their local markets and concentrating on hiring the best quality temps they can find. A reputation for high quality in turn boosts franchisee volumes and attracts new franchisees to the Uniforce marketing organization. By remixing a common strategy element—namely services to franchisees—Uniforce has found a potent source of innovative marketing.

Innovation Based on Meeting Customer Needs

Many companies pursue innovation in a classic marketing textbook fashion. That is, they discover unmet market needs and then develop products or reposition existing products to fill them. Black & Decker is a great example of this approach. For many years it has uncovered the unmet needs of do-it-yourselfers and then engineered product offerings to meet those needs, from battery-powered drills to its trademarked portable work bench. Its newest product, a cordless electric lawn mower with a rechargeable battery, appeals to environmentally sensitive consumers who don't want to pollute the air with gasoline fumes. Black & Decker has in recent years pursued this variation of innovation to launch household products that fit new needs and meet changing values. These have included spacesaver appliances such as coffeemakers as well as automatic shut-off irons.

While Black & Decker's innovations have required engineered products with new features, companies such as Procter & Gamble are masters at repositioning products to satisfy needs. For instance, after Procter & Gamble acquired Richardson-Vicks, it repositioned Pepto-Bismol, a well-established stomach upset remedy, as a treatment for traveller's diarrhea. It has also repositioned its acquired moisturizer brand, Oil of Olay, for younger women.

Utilizing this pathway to innovation requires astute market segmentation and market research so that the company understands when groups of customers within a total marketing spectrum have distinct needs. Levi Strauss, having spotted the need for men to loosen up and dress down more, developed baggier cotton twill pants. Levi's launched Dockers, its new casuals, and sold $400 million of them to older, paunchier customers. Athletic shoe manufacturers such as Nike, L.A. Gear, and Reebok today offer different shoe designs based on function and fashion; a wide range of styles is available for tennis, jogging, cycling, aerobics, and basketball in a blizzard of different fashion-enhancing colors, fabrics, and logos.

An unfilled need can be based on geographic considerations in addition to life-style, demographics, or other criteria. Wal-Mart has been a great success by targeting small-town America. Key-Corp[5] has expanded its banking services to cover low-population towns such as Troy, Idaho (population 820), and Gig Harbor, Washington (population 2,429), that lack such services. This tactic has proved very successful financially. KeyCorp tripled its assets between 1986 and 1990 to $15 billion and earnings doubled from their level four year earlier, to $317 million.

In addition to exploiting untapped needs of customers in geographically isolated areas, companies that pursue this pathway to innovation use two other variations. One is to attract customers by enhancing services. For instance, Pacific Bank offers personal and business services, such as sending a car for customers who need transportation to get to the bank, hand-delivering check reorders to customers' residences, and training the employees of its banking clients in sound bookkeeping practices. The Ritz-Carlton Hotel in Boston enhances its guest hotel services by offering custom-designed rooms for children that adjoin the parents' room. In the children's room are arts and crafts supplies, televisions, VCRs, a stereo, toys, and childproof power outlets.

The second variation on this "need-satisfying" strategy is to assist customers in gaining fuller benefits from the company's products. Skyline Displays, Inc.,[6] of Minneapolis manufactures and sells trade show booths. Recognizing that up to 40 percent of first-time trade show exhibitors do not repeat as booth users, Skyline decided to teach its customers how to exploit such booths for maximum advantage. It conducts trade-show workshops in various U.S. cities and uses workbooks, videos, and audiotapes for its customer education sessions.

Starbuck is a specialty coffee retailer that began by selling select coffee beans for at-home brewing. It now enhances its customers' use of such beans by selling brewing equipment, grinders, espresso machines, and cappuccino makers through an extremely knowledgeable sales staff. In fact, 20 percent of sales in Starbucks' sixty-three outlets now consist of such hardware.

Examples of Innovating by Filling Needs

Two companies whose pattern of growth and profitability owe their success to the pursuit of the axis of innovation are Church and Dwight Company of Princeton, New Jersey, and Aluminum Company of America (Alcoa).

Church and Dwight is the maker of Arm & Hammer baking soda. Since 1846 the company has expanded its sales by finding new unfilled needs for its sodium bicarbonate in the yellow box. Refined from mineral salts in Wyoming, the product was first sold as baking soda. With 1989 sales of $388 million, it has found even more niche uses. It is filling needs for deodorizing refrigerators, cleaning drains, polishing silver, stripping paint, reducing toxic emissions from gas power plants, neutralizing acid in swimming pools, and cutting lead contamination in town water supplies. It can even be used to clean teeth! These new need-fulfilling uses have helped Church and Dwight grow at a rate of 16 percent a year between 1985 and 1990.

Alcoa[7] has increased sales from $7 billion in 1987 to $11 billion in 1989 as the direct result of listening to customers' ideas on how aluminum can help them lower the cost and weight of their products. Beverage cans, once more than 60 percent steel, are today 97 percent aluminum. Not only has Alcoa increased its penetration of beverage can manufacture, it has met new needs for products such as lightweight yet strong beverage bottle caps. It was Alcoa, for instance, that convinced can makers that easy-opening aluminum cans could boost can sales for beverages generally compared to bottles. As Alcoa sought out new customer needs, it discovered them in both the food and dairy industries. Aluminum is widely used today for packaging products from frozen pies and yogurt to frozen cinnamon rolls and vegetable shortening. Since Alcoa's sales are in base aluminum to the packagers, many of its initiatives to innovate have required it to convince its customers' customers of the merits of aluminum closure systems and containers, as when it helped canners convince consumers of the advantages of the easy-open end feature in freeing consumers from carrying around a portable can opener.

Innovation Based on Creative Imagination

Certain businesses such as book publishing, television, music recording, and computer software believe that creativity and creative ideas provide the hydraulics for growth. These are businesses in which no business basis exists without the original creation of writers, film makers, musicians, and computer programmers. The products of such industries often must be unique each time out and are frequently crafted entirely from the world of imagination. Fashion, for example, is often a product of a designer's inner vision transformed into a garment's style and "look." The distribution of films and television programs requires new products that must be created entirely from scratch year in and year out. Pursuing this form of innovation requires a management team strong in creativity and the management of creative people.

Few companies have been able to tap the world of imagination with greater commercial success than the Walt Disney Company[8] under the creative management of CEO Michael Eisner (former president of Paramount Studios) and president Frank Wells (former vice-chairman of Warner Brothers). From 1984 to 1990, the company grew more than 20 percent a year in sales and 50 percent a year in profits. Its return on stockholder's equity in the same period rose from 8 percent to 23 percent, while its stock price went from less than $25 a share in 1984 to more than $130 a share in 1990. Disney has exploited its imagination-based assets by diversifying them in several directions and supplementing them with new ideas. Figure 2-3 illustrates the growth in Disney's imagination-based assets since 1984. Each of its growth tactics has worked well. Disney's films once generated 3 percent of the film industry's total revenues; in 1990 its share was 19 percent. Disney theme parks have gone global, and its hotel holdings now rank in size alongside major chains. Its consumer products went from $110 million in 1984 to more than $400 million in 1989; within this division its retail stores now number more than sixty across the United States. What Disney has done is to find a way to exploit a steady stream of new ideas with a great deal of fiscal discipline—strong attention to cost controls, operating margins, and sensible (not overreaching) capital expenditures. For instance, Disney's movie studios turn out films for an average of $14 million apiece, compared to an industry average of $18 million. Disney stores sell $700 a square foot compared to most mall gift shop sales of $250 a square foot. Its stores' operating profit margins of 15 percent are better than those of outstanding retailers such as The Limited. Disney theme parks yield operating margins of 30 percent despite ploughing back profits into new attractions each year.

Pursuing innovation based upon pure imagination is a risky course of action; hit movies are not easy to turn out consistently (as companies such as Twentieth-Century Fox have discovered). When managed with commonsense financial discipline by very creative people, imagination can be a winning pathway for innovation.

Consider the case of software, a business that is considered highly creative and that includes many small entrepreneurial companies. (In fact, engineering software has been compared to looking for a black cat in a dark room.) However, the Japanese are making serious attempts to engineer and "manufacture" software, a business and technology usually considered unmanageable.[9] While most companies believe that software is best produced by small, loose, "job shop" companies that resemble a craft or cottage business, the Japanese are making serious eforts to systematize their programming productivity. Toshiba, NEC, Fujitsu, NIPPON Telephone and Telegraph, and Mitsubishi are all trying to recycle computer software codes so that software need not be produced from scratch each and every time. For example, half of Toshiba's software for 1985 was produced from recycled computer programs, which had been stored in fifty program line modules in a massive computer software library. Clearly the Japanese are attempting to standardize a business heretofore considered a product of creativity. They are mimicking Disney's application of engineering to its imagination-based products and attempting to make innovating along this pathway less risky and unpredictable (software production often lags be-

(text continues on page 63)

Figure 2-3. Imagination-based asset growth: Walt Disney Company (1984–1990).

Core Asset	Original Business	Diversified Business—to Grow Original Business
Theme Parks and Resorts	Disneyland Disneyworld/Epcot	Tokyo Disneyland (Japan) Euro Disneyland (France) Disney-MGM Studio Theme Park (Florida) Hotels (20,000 rooms)
Film-Making Studio	Films for Children Disney Television Show Cartoons	Films for Adults (Touchstone Pictures) Films for Families (*Roger Rabbit*) Disney Channel Videos of Kids' Classics Records/Compact Discs of Disney Songs
Mickey Mouse and Cartoon Characters	Mickey Mouse Watches Mickey Mouse T-Shirts Mickey Mouse Stuffed Animals	More Licensed Products Gift Stores in Malls Gift Catalogs Mickey Mouse Magazine Minnie Mouse Line of Dolls/Clothing Computer Software Games

(continues)

Figure 2-3. (*continued*)

New Core Assets	

Mickey's Kitchen
(a restaurant)
	Fast-Food
	  Restaurants
	  Outside Theme
	  Parks
	Serve "Goofy"
	  Burgers,
	  "Pinocchio's"
	  Pizza, "Salads in
	  Wonderland,"
	  "Donald Duck"
	  Fruit Juice

---

hind hardware placements and incurs unanticipated cost over-runs, and the software doesn't always perform as expected).

Innovation Derived From Scientific Research

Scientific discoveries are often the propellant for certain companies' innovation. For example, DuPont has grown through innovative discoveries in basic polymer chemistry and fibers, and Corning's growth has been fueled by scientific exploitation of glass, from Corning Ware to glass fiber-optic cable for the transmission of telecommunications. These companies spend heavily on research and development and pioneer projects whose commercial success is often unassured. They believe that invention can move their companies forward, and they have a great deal of patience in trying to find niche applications for their basic discoveries. This has certainly been the case for DuPont, with its Nylon, Teflon, and Kevlar. For instance, DuPont worked very closely with Reebok to design a new athletic shoe that could exploit DuPont's "Elvajoy" polymer (the Pump Court Victory tennis shoe) as a direct challenger to Nike's air-filled shoes.

Small companies that excel at scientific exploitation often must combine efforts with larger organizations that possess greater marketing or manufacturing expertise. For instance, Genentech, a microbiology-based company expert at basic DNA molecular research, joined with Eli Lilly, the pharmaceutical giant, to market its genetically engineered insulin; Genentech provided the basic research into recombinant DNA technology while Eli Lilly produced and marketed the product of these scientific endeavors.[10]

Zeiss: Pursuing Innovation via Science

Zeiss[11] is a German manufacturer, headquartered in Oberkochen, whose existence and continued success flows from innovative scientific discoveries in the area of optical instruments. With sales exceeding 4.4 billion deutsche marks and 32,250 employees (25,000 in Germany), Zeiss dominates the global sale of optical instruments such as binoculars, microscopes, astronomical telescopes, planetariums, submarine periscopes, optical equipment for medicine, mapmaking and surveying instruments, camera lenses, "night-vision" instruments for military use, thermal cameras, and measuring machines. Zeiss also makes spectacle frames and lenses.

The company, founded in the 1860s, represented the combined scientific genius of Ernst Abbe, a university mathematics and science lecturer, and Carl Zeiss, a skilled craftsman of microscopes. Abbe pioneered the optics principles that Zeiss was able to put into commercial production, thereby gaining worldwide leadership in microscopes. Joined in the 1880s by Otto Schott, an expert in glass-smelting sciences, Zeiss produced a diverse range of optical instrumentation.

Zeiss's dedication to science includes having very large numbers of its work force drawn from the best universities and technical schools in Germany. The lens on the camera first carried on the moon by Neil Armstrong was a Zeiss; in 1983, when the first spacelab photographed Earth from 250 kilometers in space, it used an aerial survey camera from Zeiss. Up to 8,000 manhours go into the production of just one star-gazing planetarium, each of which costs millions of deutsche marks (more than twenty-five countries use Zeiss planetariums). Zeiss has grown continuously by its scientific discoveries. Its night-vision instruments can amplify light 80,000 times, and the X-ray telescope on satellites equipped with a Zeiss mirror has the flattest mirror surface ever developed—within the width of an iron atom of being perfectly flat.

Innovation Through Functional Excellence

Achieving excellence in a specific function of management provides the source of innovation for many companies. Benetton, an apparel retailer and manufacturer with global reach, is innovative in its management of information. Its retail-to-plant information system allows it to make just-in-time decisions about manufacturing the styles and colors of clothing that are moving the fastest off its franchised store shelves. Wrigley Gum, based in Chicago, reached more than $1 billion (sales) in 1989 and grew by rates of 13 percent and 22 percent in sales and profits respectively, compounded annually from 1985 to 1989. It accomplished this by its functional excellence in merchandising—a combination of clever packaging, value pricing, branding, and in-store display. For instance, in 1987, when Wrigley introduced its five-piece gum pack for twenty-five cents, compared to the industry standard of seven pieces for thirty-five cents, its sales jumped so strongly it dropped its seven-piece packs completely. Its subsidiary Amurol has the best merchandising in the kid's gum business for bubble gums and novelty gums, using licensed characters such as the Teenage Mutant Ninja Turtles.

Rolls-Royce has built and sustained its business by functional expertise in engineering, whereas Frito-Lay dominates the snack-food market in North America because of its functional excellence in logistics; its store-door delivery system of 9,000 truck route salespeople are as disciplined as an army in covering their 300,000 outlets per week. The company guarantees that its products get prime selling space exposure in retail stores as well as assuring product freshness and consistent display for Frito-Lay's new brands and flavors store by store. Without its logistics system, Frito-Lay could not have extended its brands in as controlled and successful a way as it has done. Its "cool ranch" flavored Doritos snack increased the company's total sales by $200 million, a jump of 20 percent in its billion-dollar snack food business.

Functional expertise that provides a basis for innovation is not always narrowly based. McDonald's, for example, has functional expertise in five key areas—site selection, high-quality service, new menu offerings, high-caliber advertising, and excellent employee communication. By carefully exploiting its broad spread of talents, it has emerged as dominant in its market, surpassing Burger King and Burger Chef, both of whom had market shares equal to McDonald's in the 1970s.[12] PepsiCo in recent years has concentrated on refining its functional expertise in two areas to keep its innovation alive—developing sales specialists in bottler relations and trade promotion specialists in its marketing ranks.

Using Functional Excellence for Innovation: Procter & Gamble

For a company to be able to use functional excellence as a springboard for innovation, it must clearly understand the specific skills and know-hows that comprise the function so it can apply them to new marketing opportunities. For instance, a company like Procter & Gamble, whose functional excellence is in consumer packaged-goods marketing, must understand what skills and talents make up this successful functional speciality. Figure 2-4 illustrates the constituent parts of Procter & Gamble's packaged-goods marketing function expertise.

Procter & Gamble is very knowledgeable about the skills required to turn brands such as Tide, Head & Shoulders, Crest, and Pampers into world-beaters. In each case it has correctly targeted the brand through market segmentation and research, named the brand and packaged it in an appealing way, pumped ad money and promotions into the media and trade to attract buyers and users, and leveraged its distribution channels to the maximum. So skilled is Procter & Gamble at this game that it was able to take this well-established formula and apply it to brands acquired from others such as Richardson-Vicks (which it purchased) and inject new life into them. For instances, Pepto-Bismol was retargeted for uses such as travellers' diarrhea, and Oil of Olay was retargeted to young women; spin-off versions of the brand were developed for women with sensitive skin and pushed through the same vast Procter & Gamble distribution system.[13]

Because, over many years, Procter & Gamble has identified and refined the skills it needs to be functionally excellent, it is

Figure 2-4. The skill-building blocks of packaged-goods marketing excellence: Procter & Gamble.

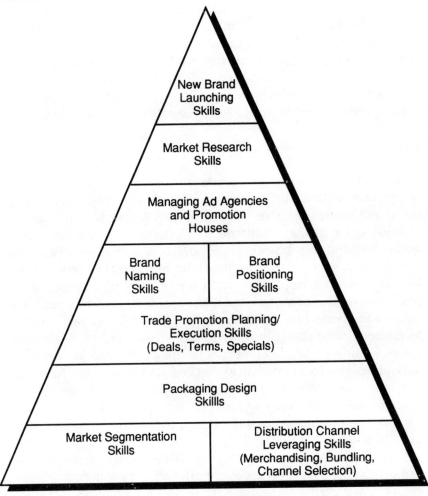

able to innovate across multiple markets, from over-the-counter stomach remedies such as Metamucil to toiletries such as Old Spice, which it acquired from American Cyanamid. Its managers' skills have also proven transferrable across geographic zones. After Procter & Gamble merged with Blendax, a German health and beauty products maker, and Perfumeria Phebo, a Brazilian cosmetics company, it successfully exploited its functional expertise to innovate with its newly acquired brands. The complex synergy of the many skills mastered by Procter & Gamble make it a difficult competitor to surpass; to beat Procter & Gamble's functional expertise, a rival must have mastered all of its skills, which is a very tall order indeed. As markets "de-massify" into more and more specialized niches, the skills embedded in Procter & Gamble's organization can provide for fertile innovation in new products, line extensions, or repositioned brands, whether these are acquired or "organically" grown by Procter & Gamble itself.

Pursuing Multiple Pathways

While most companies have a bias in their corporate culture that favors one or another variant of innovation, truly outstanding companies usually pursue multiple pathways simultaneously.

3M, for instance, simultaneously pursues four different pathways to innovation. It finds unmet needs and engineers products to fill them, such as putting its nightime reflective materials on bicycle tires in Europe using a product originally designed for road signs. The company spends considerable funds on basic science to create new technologies such as its microwoven fiber technology used for Thinsulate-brand insulation and Scotchbrite floor-cleaning pads. 3M combines technologies such as adhesives and abrasives to create sticky-backed sanding discs for body shops and industry. And the company pursues functional excellence in manufacturing—in factories that pursue low-cost strategies for the production of videotapes, packaging tape, and other key 3M lines.

While Canon is core-technology driven in its innovative practices, it too moves down other pathways. Its autofocus 35mm cameras attracted new camera users and so met previously unnoticed needs in customers that other offerings had not met.

Hallmark is functionally excellent in the retailing, distribution, and printing of thousands of different greeting cards, but its innovation also springs from the pure imagination of creating new card categories, such as nonoccasion cards, which broadened the entire market for greeting cards.

DuPont's primary innovation pathway continues to be scientific discovery of core fibers. However, it also uses other innovation paths. For instance, it has been very skilled at finding new customers for its fiber Kevlar, including tire companies and makers of bulletproof vests for police teams. American Express, while differentiating itself by innovatively mixing the same marketing elements as its rivals Visa and MasterCard, also innovates via functional excellence in direct marketing; for instance, it has launched new businesses, such as selling insurance by direct mail.

Innovation and Competitive Advantage

Regardless of whether a business uses its core technologies, scientific research, or some other axis as its source of innovation, it is imperative that it channel this innovativeness into a competitive advantage. Whatever innovation springs forth—whether it is an idea for a new retail store format, a repositioned consumer brand, a basic new material, or a new use for a product or service—management will find that it does a company little good to be innovative if it cannot be *distinctly* innovative; it is only by being distinct that it can set itself apart from its competitors. The innovation must have a *differentiating value* on a relative basis, apart from any absolute merits inherent in the innovation.

For example, it does no good for Corning to innovate in new glass materials if it garners no advantages over rivals from such discoveries. Wal-Mart's innovativeness in serving small town U.S.A. is useful to it only so long as it does this better than Sears, Target, or other chain-store rivals. Black & Decker's pursuit of innovation through newly featured tools and appliances serving untapped customer needs would be useless if its innovations were rapidly mimicked by Sunbeam, Makita, or other key competitors. It is in the clever *management* of innovation that competitive advantage can be sustained.

A major study of Britain's most admired companies[14] concluded that it was the combination of innovativeness and sensible management and a long-term emphasis on quality that set apart the most admired companies. Managements that squandered innovative ideas in favor of incoherent strategies and fiscally irresponsible acquisitions or other nonfocused diversifications were unable to sustain competitive advantages in the longer term. Saatchi and Saatchi, an advertising agency, and Next, an apparel retailer, were cited as highly innovative but ranked poorly on management criteria; both are in serious financial difficulty. McDonald's innovativeness has been harnessed since the mid-sixties into a competitive advantage that has sustained more than 100 straight quarters of earnings growth prior to 1991. Analysis strongly suggests that a company must know not only which pathway of innovation to pursue but apply talented focused management to the problem of maximizing the yield from its innovation. It is the second factor, as much as the first, that sets apart the Sonys, Disneys, Procter & Gambles, 3Ms, and Black & Deckers of this world.

Notes

1. C. N. Manning, "The End of Lockstep Marketing," *McKinsey Quarterly* (Winter 1990), p. 97.
2. For an excellent write-up on how Sony developed new niches for its products, see Brian Bagot, "Sony's Niche Knack," *Marketing and Media Decisions* (March 1989), pp. 102–103. Also see "Sony Wins Race for First Portable Digital Audio Tape," *Toronto Star* (September 22, 1990). For a corporate profile, see Nigel Cope, "Sony: Walkman's Global Stride," *Business* (U.K.) (March 1990), pp. 52–61.
3. *Designing for Product Success* (Boston: Design Management Institute), pp. 22–23.
4. See "A Long Way From Hell's Kitchen," *Forbes* (July 9, 1990), pp. 59–60, for a profile of Uniforce.
5. L. Jereski, "Small Towns Add Up to Big Banking for Key Corp," *Business Week* (April 30, 1990), p. 104.
6. Jay Finegan, "Reach Out and Teach Someone," *Inc.* Magazine (October 1990), p. 114.
7. For a thorough write-up on Alcoa's innovative customer need-filling strategies, see T. Benson, "Beyond Niche Marketing," *Industry Week* (September 17, 1990), pp. 16–19.
8. For profiles of Disney, see Christopher Knowlton, "How Disney Keeps the Magic Going," *Fortune*, (December 4, 1989),

pp. 111–132; Kathleen Kerwin and Antonio Fins, "Disney Is Looking Just a Little Fragilistic," *Business Week* (June 25, 1990), pp. 52–54; "Disney and the World of Foodservice," *Nations Restaurants* (May 28, 1990), p. 1; "Walt Disney Launches a Line of Minnie Mouse Products," *Advertising Age* (August 27, 1990), p. 36.

9. A write-up on software factories in Japan (called Sofutouea Kojo) can be found in S. Maital, "Why Not Software Factories?" *Across the Board* (October 1990), pp. 5–6.

10. Regis McKenna, *The Regis Touch* (Reading, Mass.: Addison Wesley, 1985), p. 76.

11. Alan Purkiss, "Zeiss Buries a Family Feud," *Business* (U.K.) (July 1990), pp. 79–82.

12. Robert Irvin, "Focus on Core Skills," *Boardroom Reports* (May 1, 1990), p. 7.

13. Zachary Schiller, "Procter & Gamble Is Adding New Spice to Old Spice," *Business Week* (July 9, 1990), pp. 32–33.

14. "Britain's Most Admired Companies," *The Economist* (September 9, 1989), pp. 87–90.

3

Access to Markets: Distribution Channel Management

A company with the best distribution system and the best service will win all the marbles—because you can't keep an advantage in other areas for long.

Lee Iacocca
Iacocca

Distribution channels are often the major engine driving a company's growth. Compaq Computer made it into the Fortune 500 faster than any other company, in part because of its solid dealer network. Frito-Lay dominates the marketing of snack foods because its store-door distribution system is second to none. Steelcase's office furniture distributors provide the stability and market access it needs to lead in an otherwise fragmented marketplace.

When Apple Computer moved to revive its U.S. sales, its first step was to patch up its dealer relations, which had fallen into disarray. Apple's dealers resented Apple's direct sale of computers to large Fortune-500–size customers. In order to shore up dealer relations, Apple is turning over its corporate sales to its local dealers. Apple's largest dealer customer, Computerland Corporation, views this move very positively, believing that it provides dealers with enhanced credibility in the eyes of end-using computer buyers.[1]

The company with the finest distribution network often wins the battle for market share and can substantially block a rival from penetrating a market. For instance, when Komatsu,[2] the Japanese manufacturer of heavy machinery such as forklifts and dump trucks, tried to gain a strong foothold in America, it attempted to entice Clark Equipment's seventy independent dealers across the United States to drop Clark's line of forklifts in favor of its own. Clark improved its product offering by buying the Euclid dump truck division of Daimler-Benz to match Komatsu's one–two punch of forklifts *and* dump trucks. In so doing, it was able to hold the loyalty of its dealers and severely cripple Komatsu's attempt at market penetration.

A company's choice of distribution channels plays a key role in positioning its products. Two wines, identically aged, bottled, and made from the same grapes, are positioned completely differently if one is sold in a supermarket and the other in a gourmet food store. The same is true for two identical personal computers sold in Kmart and Businessland. The Kmart computer is positioned more as a toy, whereas the other is more likely to be seen as a business productivity tool.

How Distribution Channels Work

A company's ability to gain market access through distribution channels depends upon its understanding of how the channels operate. Figure 3-1 shows how a manufacturer of pharmaceuticals in Japan goes to market. As the diagram illustrates, drug companies can reach end consumers of ethical pharmaceuticals along at least six distinct pathways. These include wholesalers, retailers, and intermediaries such as hospitals and clinics. If a company trying to penetrate the Japanese pharmaceuticals market does not understand each of these pathways, including the percentage of product that finds its way along each path, the company won't stand a chance of optimizing the sale of its ethical drugs to potential consumers.

Distribution channels are becoming more complex. Today, a consumer can bank at a 7-Eleven convenience store, buy auto parts at a drugstore, take out a mortgage at Sears, and order a

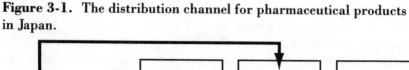

Figure 3-1. The distribution channel for pharmaceutical products in Japan.

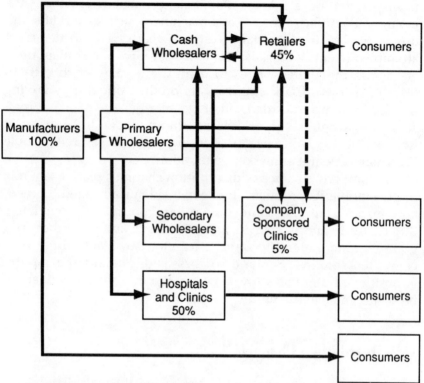

Source: Roger W. Dace, "Exporting to Japan—Key Factors for Success," *The Quarterly Review of Marketing* (August 1990), p. 3.

Mother's Day gift with a home computer. A florist's largest competitor is likely to be the supermarket down the street, while the supermarket's largest competitor may be the cluster of fast-food restaurants across the road. Hotel chains are getting into retirement and health care facilities, and credit card companies compete with traditional agents for insurance business by using mail-order selling. Even Cessna aircraft is opening retail stores to sell aviation gifts, sportswear, pilot supplies, and flight lessons.

The most important innovations in marketing channels in recent years include (1) the huge growth of both direct marketing and electronic shopping; (2) the accelerated proliferation of franchised operations; (3) the strengthening of retailer-owned cooperative wholesalers; (4) the spread of specialized niche retailers; and (5) the rapid evolution of contract buying systems in industrial distribution.

Channel Changes

Direct Marketing

Consumers today buy $200 billion worth of all manner of goods from mail-order companies, catalogs, television shopping channels, and direct factory outlets. Nonstore selling has grown as households become busier, as credit card usage becomes more widespread and accepted, and as the quality of goods sold by mail, telephone, and television improves. Catalog sales for department stores such as Sears and J. C. Penney exceed $1 billion a year; more than 10,000 catalogs exist in the United States, as mail-order specialists sell products as diverse as computers and parts for antique automobiles. L. L. Bean's sales by mail order grew from under $5 million a year in the 1960s to more than $300 million in the 1980s. Quill Company, one of America's most successful stationers, sells office supplies by mail and phone order across North America. Its mailings include one million catalogs *a month* to selected offices of varying sizes. Even hotel chains such as Marriott and Loews use telemarketers to sell weekend or convention packages to customers. As this distribution channel increases in sophistication and maturity, it is becoming the subject of intense scrutiny by legislators wishing to protect the consumer's privacy from the unwanted incursions of telephone or "junk mail" sales campaigns.

Another form of direct marketing is the factory outlet selling high-profile "signature" brands such as Ralph Lauren's Polo, Christian Dior, and Sergio Valente. In New England, there are more than 600 factory outlets, selling clothing[3] as well as cosmetics, wallets, belts, shoes, tableware, furniture, lingerie, linen, rainwear, and even tools. More than 160 factory outlets are clustered in Freeport, Maine, alone. More than 200 factory outlet malls are operating across the United States; one of North America's busiest is in Orlando, Florida. A factory outlet is no longer located in a dark recess near the loading dock of the manufacturer's plant; it is a roomy, attractive store carrying mostly first-class merchandise in all lines and sizes. These outlets often operate seven days a week with well-trained staffs, and they take credit cards. They are successfully meeting the growing societal desire for fashionable namebrand merchandise at discount prices.

Franchised Channels of Distribution

So many businesses have now been franchised that it is becoming difficult to name a business or service that has not been or could not be franchised. Over one-third of all retail sales are now franchised, and this figure will rapidly rise to one-half at current projected growth rates. Once highly fragmented, Mom-and-Pop businesses, from dry cleaning to real estate brokerages have been systematically franchised in the United States, Canada, and Europe (see Figure 3-2).

Franchising unites the entrepreneurship of the small-business owner with the capital and professional marketing polish of the franchiser. By bridging gaps in owners' experience and capitalization, franchising has proven to be a powerful formula for overcoming fragmentation in businesses from household maid service to funeral home operation.

An idea, when franchised properly, can have stunningly rapid impacts on marketing channels. Oil companies now can market enormous quantities of motor oil via quick-lube shops. Bedding manufacturers have a new big channel customer in franchised no-frill motel chains. Even educational book publishers and toymakers are presented with a new channel for their sales in the rapidly-growing business of franchised child daycare chains.

Much of this innovation has come about from outsiders to the industry. For example, quick-lube shops were made successful by people from outside the established oil-company auto-service industry, and it was not the large national hotel/motel chains that franchised successful no-frill motel chains such as "Super 8."

Figure 3-2. Small businesses transformed by franchising.

Language Schools	**Fitness Clubs**	**Antique Refinishing**
House Painting	**Disaster Restoration**	**Carpet Cleaning**
Plumbing	**Real Estate Agencies**	**Drain Cleaning**
Window Glazing/	**Travel Agencies**	**Dry Cleaning**
Repair	**Restaurants**	**Bridal Wear and**
Swimming Pool	**Maid Service**	**Formal Wear**
Contractors	**Legal Services**	**Artist Supplies**
Tax Services	**Quick-Print**	**Bathroom**
Insurance	**Businesses**	**Equipment**
Courier Services	**Beauty Products**	**Key Cutting**
Auctioneering	**Accountancies**	**Shoe Repair**
Debt Collections	**Business Training**	**Pet Stores**
Rust-Proofing	**Camp Grounds and**	**Picture Framing**
Oil Changes	**Fun Parks**	**Funeral Services**
Brakes, Mufflers,	**Food Boutiques**	**Water Conditioning**
Transmissions,	**Eye Care**	**Tool Rental Outlets**
Tune-Ups	**Lawn Care**	**Appliance Repair**
Car and Truck	**Pest Control**	**Hearing Aid Stores**
Rentals	**Chimney Cleaning**	**Career Counselling**
Day Care		

For a write-up on franchising, see Kenneth G. Hardy and Allan J. Magrath, *Marketing Channel Management: Strategic Planning and Tactics* (Glenview, Ill.: Scott, Foresman & Co., 1988), pp. 361–371.

Retailer-Owned Cooperatives

Innovative marketing channels often emerge when channel members link different activities. Take the case of retailer-owned cooperative wholesalers in hardware trades. Until the 1960s, the channel was not a very large part of total hardware sales in the United States, totalling certainly less than 10 percent. But twenty-odd years later, this has radically changed. Over 24,000 hardware retailers belong to retailer-owned cooperative wholesale groups such as True Value Hardware (Cotter & Company), Ace Hardware, Hardware Wholesalers Incorporated, and Handy Hardware. With the help of these groups, the independent hardware retail dealer has survived, despite having to compete with giants like Sears, Kmart, and large home-building-center chains such as Home Depot.

The reason these retailer-owned cooperative wholesalers have proven a match for both mass-merchandising vertical chains and traditional hardware wholesalers is their ability to run cost-competitive operations and to be innovative in merchandising. By integrating retailers and wholesalers in one organization, the retailer-owned cooperative wholesaler realizes many advantages over an independent unaffiliated wholesaler. It can cut its selling expenses because there is no need to generate demand when there are loyal retailers who place regular orders. The co-op wholesaler's buying activities can be more precise because its retail members' orders are more predictable, and its inventory control is superior to that of an independent unaffiliated whole-saler. Usually coop-owned wholesalers do not need to extend as much credit as do independents. Order handling costs are re-duced because the co-op can pressure the retailers to order on a more systematic basis since the retailers are linked to the co-op. Average order sizes can be kept closer to the ideal in order to minimize operating costs. Because of retailer loyalty to the co-op wholesaler, it is also easier for the wholesaler to test demand for new products, and occasionally sell off slow movers, among various retail co-op members. Established order schedules im-posed by the coop-owned wholesaler also can cut its delivery costs compared to competitive, unaffiliated independent whole-salers.

Retailer-owned wholesalers can develop promotion packages of great interest to all retail members, as well as implement common brand identifications for store signing, layout, and re-tailer advertising. Such arrangements also lead to the promotion of strong private labels between the wholesaler and retailer mem-bers. In this respect, such benefits confer upon the retailers the appearance of having almost a chain-like uniformity of image. In effect, these quasi-integrated channel members enjoy the best of both worlds; they enjoy the advantages of corporate chain identi-ties and large-scale buying economies, as well as the advantages of independents, who have the flexibility to respond rapidly to changes in local market conditions.

Specialized Niche Retailers

The high per capita incomes of many Americans has led to opportunities for specialized retailers of all kinds. Paint and wallpaper stores have repositioned their offerings as decorating centers. Lumberyards are home-building centers that dispense products and advice to all sorts of do-it-yourselfers. Upscale fashion boutiques have cut into the department and discount store sales of dress apparel, shoes, handbags, casual sports clothing, and fashion accessories.

The increasing fragmentation of markets has led retail store chains to position themselves to attract specific populations— singles, young marrieds with no children, single-parent households, empty-nester and over-50 households. And these chains, such as The Limited, Nordstrom, and Toys "R" Us, are experiencing great success. Figure 3-3 illustrates the high rate of growth in sales at specialty chains compared to U.S. department stores.

New retail formats within formerly single-format classes of

Figure 3-3. Selected specialty store growth compared with U.S. department stores.

Average U.S. Department Store Growth in 1989: −2.3%

Specialty Chain	Parent Company	Type of Specialty	Percentage Sales Gains 1989	Number of Stores
Toys "R" Us	Independent	Toys	19.7	404
The Limited	Independent	Apparel	14.2	3,168
Kinney Shoes	Woolworth	Shoes	18.2	3,604
Radio Shack	Tandy	Electronics	2.5	4,821
Circuit City	Independent	Electronics	21.9	149
Marshalls	Melville	Apparel	10.6	347
T. J. Maxx	TJM	Apparel	12.9	352
The Gap	Independent	Apparel	26.8	960
Petrie Shoes	Independent	Apparel	3.2	1,569
U.S. Shoe	U.S.S.	Apparel	7.2	1,721

Source: "Re-Thinking Retail: Making It in the 90s," *Breakthrough*, a communique from Backer, Spievogel, Bates in Toronto (November 1990).

trade are common; for instance, in food retailing there are standard supermarkets, box stores with limited assortments, combination stores (drug and grocery/hardware), warehouse stores, and superwarehouses stores, all selling groceries and some nonfoods. This same scenario applies to very narrow product category sellers. There are warehouse electronics stores, warehouse toy stores, warehouse drug stores, and even warehouse "big man" clothing stores.

This change in existing patterns of marketing distribution has had a major impact on suppliers. Demands of chain buyers for merchandising programs, price specials, and deals of all sorts now *vary depending on the store format* because their retail selling space configurations and profit-making formulas vary so much. Point-of-purchase advertising programs are very difficult to standardize in today's retailing.

Contract Buying Systems in Industrial Channels

Technological change such as computerization affects the abilities of members of a distribution channel to transact business, and this creates new pathways to sales. For instance, electronic banking using automated teller machines represents a new transaction pathway.

In industrial markets, for example, distributors are now often linked directly with key customers by computer-to-computer ordering. This technological breakthrough allows for new marketing channel relationships such as *contract supply systems,* in which the end customer can order from the distributor on a just-in-time basis and significantly reduce on-hand inventories. This system allows the end customer to save space and avoid the costs of product obsolescence, product handling, storage, insurance, and administration. Such systems-contracting relationships are so strong that the distributor often holds greater influence over end customers' purchases than its supplier. A manufacturer who wishes to bypass the distributor to sell the end customer directly would find the end customer unwilling to forgo the benefits of the contract system.

Many automotive assembly plants receive contract supply on just-in-time required parts and supplies from distributors. For example, Cameron and Barkley Co., a large U.S. distributor, was awarded all of GE's U.S. appliance parts replenishment business as part of a supply system contract valued at $10 million annually. The contract requires Cameron and Barkley to provide just-in-time service; it can generate on-line orders, releases, advance shipping notices, and invoices via electronic computer hookups to GE's computers.

In high-tech marketing, customers often opt to purchase turnkey systems from a system integrator, a middleman who puts together hardware and software from various sources to solve a customer's problem. For instance, Harnischfeger Engineers, Inc., (HEI) is the systems integrator subsidiary of Harnischfeger Industries, manufacturers of cranes and storage retrieval products for warehouses. HEI sells systems that fill customer needs for automated material handling, including a complete package of software and hardware sourced from numerous vendors who make components Harnischfeger Industries does not, such as controls and certain specialized conveyors. In fact, HEI normally specifies in a system only 20 percent of the components sourced from its own parent company.

Systems integrators such as HEI are just one type of new distribution channel that has grown up in response to customer demands for contract supply.

The Impact of Evolving Channel Change

The result of new channel innovations in many cases is to force manufacturers to market products in multichannel systems.[4] For instance, IBM uses a direct sales force channel to market its expensive mainframe computers to large companies, value-added resellers to sell mid-range systems, and personal computer dealers to market its smaller personal computers. This type of tiered marketing is illustrated on Figure 3-4. It is noteworthy that prior to 1981, IBM had little experience selling computers through intermediaries, preferring instead to sell all of its hardware through its own sales force. Clearly, IBM had to learn a whole new set of skills to sell through independent middlemen, whose orientation and allegiances varied from those of IBM's own sales reps.

Figure 3-4. A tiered multichannel approach: IBM.

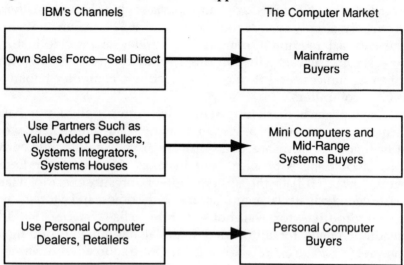

Strategic Issues

There are a number of strategic issues concerning channels that require forethought. Each can be phrased as a key question:

Is the Most Effective Channel Variety Being Used?

As markets change and products move along their product life cycles, a company must often increase the number of distribution channels it uses. Consider, for example, a manufacturer of personal computer software and accessories. As more personal computers are being sold into more and more vertical market segments, a variety of distribution channels have emerged. Computer retailers and systems houses have been joined by specialty software retailers, office stationers, catalog houses, direct mail companies, specialized national distributors, campus book stores, and numerous other value-added resellers and agents. Some of these channels cater to distinct segments of the market, while others serve overlapping users. Any software or computer accessories supplier totally absent from the various channels available risks market share losses as the market broadens and product choices proliferate. Companies must take care to move astutely to enfranchise as many different channels as the need to cover the broad market mosaic dictates; otherwise, it risks being shut out of the market. For example, Wang failed to move fast enough to enfranchise dealer channels for its personal computer, sticking with its direct sales channel far too long. By the time it made the decision to move, it found the most attractive channels already plugged with rival products, and dealers were unwilling to switch over to Wang and get behind the sale, installation, and servicing of its personal computers.

One of Britain's leading plumbing fixture manufacturers was similarly caught off guard when the do-it-yourself market developed in the United Kingdom. It found itself the confirmed market leader in plumbing wholesale channels serving contractors, but it had to play catch-up to get its products displayed and sold in the rapidly growing do-it-yourself specialized retail stores.

Figure 3-5 illustrates the impact of channel variety on one market (consumer electronics) and the rapid changes in growth prospects for each channel. A maker of VCRs or television sets must clearly keep a close watch on this information or risk being strong in the wrong channels or weak in the growing ones.

Do Channel Arrangements Guarantee Marketing Clout?

Channel clout springs from both product category clout and contractual/ownership arrangements with channels. In order to assure itself of some clout with marketing channels, a company needs to ask itself how it's doing on each of these dimensions. For instance, Procter & Gamble uses supermarkets as its dominant channel of distribution. Yet the buying power of supermarkets has been consolidated into giant chains, and checkout scanners have caused their information power about brand sales to grow explosively. This has given the chains far more power vis à vis suppliers such as Proctor & Gamble. In order to gain some added sales clout, Procter & Gamble reorganized its sales force so that one sales rep now sells multiple brands or a complete product category, such as health and beauty products or paper and personal hygiene products. (Procter & Gamble has 12 brands of detergent alone!) This selling strategy has given Procter &

Figure 3-5. Consumer electronics channels in the United States.

	Percentage of Volume Sold by Channel 1989	Percentage of Volume Forecasted by Channel 1994	Change Forecasted
Electronic Superstores	27%	32%	Up 20%
Stereo, Hi-Fi Stores	24	16	Down 33%
Discount Stores (e.g., Kmart)	10	14	Up 40%
Department Stores (e.g., Sears)	7	5	Down 30%
Catalog Showrooms	5	5	No Change
Warehouse Clubs (e.g., Price Club)	5	8	Up 40%
Other Outlets (Camera Stores, Food Stores, Furniture Stores)	22	20	Down 10%
	100%	100%	

Note: 1% of market equals: 210,000 TV Sets
25,000 Camcorders
103,000 VCRs

Source: Adapted from *Retail Home Furnishings* Magazine (May 15, 1989), pp. 75, 89.

Gamble much more clout per rep than the practice of using reps to sell only single brands in a category.

Many appliance manufacturers, such as Maytag and Hoover, have merged as a way to gain added clout with key retailer channels. Similarly, the merger of Kraft and General Foods provided added clout for these companies in several grocery food categories.

A second way a company can gain clout with its distributor

channels is to reexamine the nature of the legal arrangements between them. A manufacturer can opt to tighten its distributor agreements, to consider the possibility of formal franchising arrangements, or even to consider the buyout of key channels. Kentucky Fried Chicken, for example, is attempting to tighten its control over franchises by mandating scheduled remodelling frequencies, by eliminating perpetual automatic franchise renewals, and by restricting sale or transfers of franchises. Baume and Mercier, the Geneva-based luxury watchmaker, bought legal control of its exclusive U.S. distributor, David G. Steven, Inc., to give it a stronger market control and presence in America.

In order to gain control and ensure access to some European markets (prior to the unified market scheduled to be in place by the end of 1992), some U.S. electrical manufacturers have taken equity positions in key European distributorships. A good close look at distribution channel arrangements often turns up the need to clarify exactly what is expected of channels and what is in turn owed to the distributor by the manufacturer. Such arrangements become crucial if "gray marketing" (sales of a supplier's products by unauthorized distribution) may be present, since the enforcement of tight contracts (through warranty—service exclusivity and "trademark use clauses" for authorized distributors only) may be one of the few ways to police unauthorized distributor sales.

Does the Channel Network Have Too Many Middlemen?

One common mistake that can lead to dealer or distributor tension is for manufacturers to open up too many dealers or retailers in a specific region in its effort to achieve blanket market coverage. The presence of too many dealers can harm the whole system by inducing excessive price competition as the dealers compete for common end users. It can also result in problems in maintaining image consistency and dealer supervision.

In the cellular telephone market in the United Kingdom, British Telecom opened up an excessive number of dealers to both service burgeoning demand and hold market share. As growth slowed, the company found that it needed to cull from its dealer network those members whose servicing, selling, installation, or marketing skills were not satisfactory. Cartier, the jeweler and fragrance manufacturer, cut back its retailer network from 700 stores to 110 because its resources were stretched too thin to provide the retailers with proper marketing support.

Another reason oversaturation often occurs is that manufacturers sometimes grant selling rights for their total line to a niche distributor with a window on a very specialized market application for the manufacturer's products, even though the distributor has developed a market for only part of the line. In its search for other customers to whom it can sell the balance of the line, the new distributor then sells to customers of the manufacturer's long-established full-line distributors. This results in more market coverage on some accounts than is really required and hostility toward the manufacturer from its long-service distributors. A good rule of thumb is to establish only enough distributors so that each can expand its account scope without too much overlap with the other distributors in the area. Niche distributors with single-product-line customers should be set up and managed as such: Specialized niche distributors should earn the right to gain access to the full line only after proving they can sell the additional line items to *new* accounts, not accounts already serviced by existing distributors. Thus, General Motors is attempting to be very selective in setting up dealers for its new Saturn automobile to avoid the problem of having too many dealers chasing limited demand, driving one another broke in the process.

Do Channel Members' Functions Fit Marketing Needs?

Marketing channels perform functions for both end customers and the suppliers who enfranchise them with products. When marketing or sales results appear to be off target, the supplier needs to stand back and ask itself if its channels are capable of performing all the tasks it requires of them and whether the channels' performance is as efficient as it should be. Perhaps the supplier itself ought to perform some tasks usually delegated to the distributor.

For instance, as its product line has become more technically complex, Compaq Computer has had a channel problem. Many of its dealers lack the sophisticated selling skills necessary to sell the more complex Systempro line. Compaq's product has more networking utility; in some cases, it has the capacity (as a file server) to compete with minicomputers selling for thousands of dollars more. Compaq must either solve this channel dilemma by assisting its dealers to assimilate new sales skills and capabilities or consider direct sale of this product to end customers. Since Compaq has always been 100 percent committed to a "dealer-only" channel, this strategy dilemma is very vexing.

IBM in Canada had a different concern. It used value-added resellers to sell midrange computers and yet didn't feel it had as much control over such independents as it desired. Nor did it need all the full-service capabilities (such as invoicing customers, carrying inventory, and shipping product) offered by value-added resellers. So IBM opted for the use of agents, giving IBM tighter pricing control; IBM performs account billing and shipping very adequately on behalf of its agents. The agent then becomes more like a member of IBM's own sales team, bringing to the company knowledge of vertical markets, widespread contacts for sales leads, and the ability to help IBM sell complete midrange systems of its computers and other system components not manufactured by IBM.

Whether a manufacturer feels its channel is overqualified to perform functions it can perform just as well itself or whether its channel has nagging functional gaps in its abilities to go to market with the manufacturers' products, companies should clearly take a look at what functions its chosen distribution should fulfill and how those functions are in fact being handled.

Is Turnover and Conflict in the Channels Acceptable?

When manufacturers constantly hire and fire dealers, they create unrest and distrust in the dealer network. In addition, they waste the precious resources they invested in training and helping these dealers. Sounder policy requires companies to consider distribution channels as real partners and to govern their actions accordingly.

A company doesn't operate its own sales force by keeping turnover high and bringing on too many new reps to train and deploy properly, so why should it do this with dealers? A periodic housecleaning of nonperforming dealers can be a good thing, but caution is required; a company should make certain such housecleanings are indeed periodic or it may drive some of its best distributors into the arms of its competitors, as their attitudes toward the company change from wholehearted support to guarded anxiety.

Conflict may also occur when a company hasn't really thought through the optimum size mix of distributors for its business. In deciding on a given mix of local independent distributors, large regionals, and large national chains, a company can create some of its own headaches. Small locally owned distributors often require that the supplier have more conflict-handling skills since flare-ups are very frequent because of the dealers' proximity to one another. Local dealers are often more problematic to motivate because it is difficult for them to separate the goals of the business (profitable long-term growth and profit retention) from their personal entrepreneurial financial goals (withdrawing too much money from the business or growing sales in order to sell the business off). Larger regional or national distributors are less subject to emotionally based conflicts because of their professional management structures and diverse, often public, shareholders. However, the conflicts they do engage in are more serious, and more total dollars are at risk each time a potential disaffection occurs (since the dollars each accounts for represent a larger percent of the total sales mix). For instance, Goodyear feels its smaller dealers are far less prone to discount their tires from large national chains such as Kmart. So Goodyear's average pricing is far superior in small accounts. A balance in dealer sizes is probably optimum; smaller entrepreneurial dealers keep the larger dealers on their toes, while the larger dealers' professionalism forces the small locals to upgrade their skills or risk falling by the wayside.

Is the Mix of Dealer Types Right?

Companies seeking optimum market coverage should be sure that they have the right mix of dealers on two dimensions: (1) general-line versus specialty dealers and (2) private family-owned versus publicly-owned distributorships. Usually a manufacturer needs a mix of general-line dealers (for whom the manufacturer's products represent only a small percentage of products carried) and specialty dealers (for whom the manufacturer's lines represent a larger share of its business). The general-line dealers bundle like products together, enabling them to service end customers who want one-stop shopping for these items. The specialist often covers a secondary part of the market in which customers have narrowly defined specialized needs and therefore seek out the specialized dealers' value-added services. For example, a company selling work gloves to industry can achieve optimum market coverage of all potential end users of gloves by using general-line safety distributors *and* specialty distributors who service welders, oil-field drilling crews, construction markets, and others.

A company's strategic choice whether to use family-owned distributorships or publicly-owned distributors can depend on which type of distribution suits its style of marketing. For example, Caterpillar, Inc. prefers to use family-owned dealerships to market its construction machinery. Its management believes the best dealers are families who have their heart and soul in the distributorship and who are highly motivated to be responsive on parts and service so critical to construction equipment buyers. Caterpillar believes publicly-owned distributors treat their distributorships more as investments than an integral twenty-four-hour-a-day hands-on service commitment.

Tactical Issues—Getting Channels to Work Effectively

Decisions on the proper channel mix, saturation level, control, functions, and variety are strategic. Each involves network design variables that can shift over time as circumstances change.

Another entire set of channel decisions involves getting the network to function smoothly, with as few bottlenecks and disharmonies as possible. There are a number of tactical questions that manufacturers can use to assess the issue of dealer or distributor efficiency and effectiveness.

Are the Channel Supports Superior to Those of the Competition?

Manufacturers usually provide a broad array of supports to dealers or distributors in addition to simply offering their products. To augment the sale of products and assure that its dealers' needs are being met, companies need to think of a portfolio of different types of supports, each of which serves a different purpose.

Figure 3-6 illustrates this portfolio approach, which requires the manufacturer to define that array of supports that is both appealing to the dealer and affordable to the manufacturer. The company should provide those supports in the most competitively unique ways. For instance, Wiremold Company's electrical division has a very creative returned-goods support. Any of its distributors can return up to 5 percent of a previous year's purchases as long as it orders twice as much inventory as it

Figure 3-6. A distributor support portfolio model.

returns. Distributors like this support because it keeps obsolete stock write-offs to a minimum and assures them that inventory dollars will be invested in fast-moving products; Wiremold likes the policy because distributors are less reluctant to order its new products when they know they can return "dead" stock.

As Figure 3-6 shows, supports can be services (logistical or transactional), financial, or interpersonal. Broadly speaking, supports range from those that build skills or capabilities (such as training) to those whose aim is to build trust and longer-lasting relationships between dealer principals and employees and the manufacturer's management and field personnel.

As a rule of thumb, communications with distributors always work best when relationships are built across each company's hierarchy at three levels—at the management level, at the field level, and at the order desk level.

Some companies' relationships with their key dealers are so good that they behave more like partnerships than a third-party supplier-distributor. For instance, Thomas and Betts[5] has a very tight working partnership with its electrical distributors. In one case, United Electric Supply of Delaware (a $50-million diversified electrical distributor), one of Thomas and Betts' electrical distributors, plays a key role in helping Thomas and Betts with its Total Quality Excellence effort. United regularly measures Thomas and Betts' efforts at supplying United with error-free shipping and invoicing. For its part, United has met with Thomas and Betts to coordinate its ordering and consolidate its airship orders into simple master orders. (United's various departments had not been coordinating their demands on Thomas and Betts, requiring United to place multiple air shipment orders for different Thomas and Betts lines on the same business day without regard to consolidated shipment savings. This waste can occur quite easily in a distributorship with 170 employees, multiple departments, and six branches scattered from Maryland to Pennsylvania.)

Good communications and distribution supports strongly bond suppliers and dealers together. In addition, creative supports offer a company "differentiating potential" to set itself apart from its rivals. Skil Corporation, a maker of saws and power tools, used its distributor council (an appointed group of spokespersons representing its top distributors) to gather product design suggestions for new products, such as its innovative new power miter saw.[6]

A creative dealer program can greatly strengthen a dealer's appeal and effectiveness with end consumers. Volkswagen AG,[7] for example, rewards its U.S. dealers' sales reps bonuses for cars sold, for which the money is accumulated and collected over a long period of time. The payout depends on the salesperson's ability to pass regular tests about Volkswagen automobiles. Final installments are withheld for a year and forfeited if the sales rep quits the dealership. In this way, Volkswagen offers an incentive to reps to remain knowledgeable about its products, to remain with its dealerships, and to reverse the chronic high turnover of car dealer sales reps that plagues the industry and damages an automaker's reputation with the buying public. A rep selling thirty cars a quarter (ten a month) forfeits $12,000 if he or she quits the Volkswagen dealership. That is a lot of money, and it forces reps to think about a career with Volkswagen instead of merely a short-term sales job.

Creative or relevant dealer supports often elicit a positive reaction from resellers. Compaq Computer got just such a reaction when it offered training classes to its 1,650 resellers on its sophisticated Systempro computers. More than 8,300 dealer personnel signed up and attended training classes only a couple of weeks after the training plan was announced.

When Lennox, a maker of air conditioning and heating units, offered its dealers an advisor to assist them in financial planning, market analysis, personnel management, and training for their dealerships, it got a positive response from 230 of its 700 dealers across the United States. Sales of Lennox's products grew at twice the industry rate in those dealerships within the total Lennox network that received the consulting services.

Does the Company Have Sensible Conflict-Resolution Methods for Working With Channels?

Few things turn off distributors more than having a problem crop up, turning for help to their supplier, and being treated, in the words of one distributor, "as if you have a disease." Companies that do not respond to dealer complaints compound the failure;

studies of dissatisfied customers show conclusively that they tell others of their poor experience, poisoning whatever well of good will had accumulated with negative word-of-mouth publicity.

One company that is trying hard to address this problem with its large retailer customers is Procter & Gamble. Multifunctional teams handle key accounts; if a retailer has a logistics problem due to late shipments, the retailer talks directly with Procter & Gamble's transportation expert. This setup quickly puts the retailer in touch with the Procter & Gamble person with the expertise to solve the retailer's problem. Procter & Gamble's former system of having a salesperson act as a go-between to sort out problems for accounts provided neither the most rapid nor the most expert attention.

Are Information Linkages With the Distributors in the Best Possible Shape?

Industrial distributors are showing a growing appetite to get inside the information system loop of their supplying manufacturers with electronic data interchange (EDI). In a national survey of 831 distributors, 16 percent were found to be already hooked up to their suppliers.

Federal Mogul, a national manufacturer of bearings, pistons, and seals, is hooked up to its distributors so that they can scan Federal's supply stock status in all forty-three of its branches on any of its 16,000 parts. Distributors can look at the same "real-time" data as a Federal Mogul employee and, using this rapid data access, determine how best to satisfy end customers' service requirements for stock.

One of the challenges for any company that wishes to keep its distributor network onside (in its fold) is to provide the crucial data it needs to help run its operation. Information linkages are one important element in this customer satisfaction equation.

Does the Design of the Price-Volume Discount Schedule and Merchandising Plan Make Sense?

The judicious redesign of price-volume discounts and volume incentive merchandising plans can go a long way toward solidifying dealer support for a manufacturer's line. Fire-King International of New Albany, Indiana, was the number-six producer of fireproof filing cabinets in 1974, and both its sales and dealer commitment to its products were waning. By 1989, sales had increased sixteen-fold (from $1 million to $16 million), and its market share had climbed to 37 percent, or number one in its industry. All of this occurred as a direct result of Fire-King's restructuring its pricing and merchandising. Fire-King introduced a prepaid freight program to make it less costly for dealers to buy its heavier, sturdier cabinets. It simplified its total line so dealers could stock fewer total models and still sell its best and fastest-selling cabinets. It priced its premium line more competitively so that dealers could sell "Cadillac cabinets for Chevrolet prices." Finally, it put together merchandise volume incentive plans in which top-selling dealers earned trip credits instead of receiving free goods "deals," as offered by Fire-King's competitors.

Any supplier wanting to motivate dealers should take a close look at all components of its step discount, from its order minimum levels to the number and scale of volume price breaks. How these are engineered determines how much inducement dealers have to move up to the next volume buying bracket. A company can also examine how to "plus" the basic structure with extra incentives built around a variety of promotional objectives, from changes in the dealer sales mix to new product promos.

Compaq Computer, for example, supplements its volume discounts to dealers with financing supports on dealer inventory and accounts receivable.

Is the Company Aligned With the Fastest-growing Dealers?

In a major study of trends among wholesalers and distributors, the Distribution Research and Education Foundation predicted that in all lines of business, the larger distribution companies were getting even larger at the expense of others, primarily as a result of acquisitions and mergers.[8] In 1990, *Industrial Distribution* magazine reported that more than 56 percent of American distributors with annual sales greater than $5 million had been approached with an acquisition offer.[9] For instance, W. W. Grainger, the largest U.S. general supply distributor at $1.5 billion in sales, bought Vonnegut Industrial Products, a $40 million specialty distributor; Kent Electronics Corporation, a Houston distributor, grew from $47 million in sales in 1989 to $200 million as it acquired other distributors from California to Minnesota.[10]

The moral in all of this is obvious—if you are a manufacturer, you must ensure that you are a preferred supplier to one of the increasingly powerful megadistributors with national reach. For instance, electronic connector manufacturers such as AMP, Molex, Belden, and 3M have all actively improved their business with Kent Electronics as its stature has grown.

This same channel issue also applies to retailing. A manufacturer of do-it-yourself hardware or tools must ensure itself of a solid standing with chains such as Home Depot or Wal-Mart if it is to achieve its overall growth or market share objectives.

Other Issues Affecting Distribution Decisions

Competing With One's Own Distribution Channels

Manufacturers eager for market growth frequently get into the distribution game themselves in competition with their own appointed resellers. For instance, both Firestone and Goodyear operate company-owned outlets that compete with their own franchised stores and independent distributors, and Hallmark Cards operates retail stores in the same shopping malls as independent card shops that carry Hallmark's card lines.

Few issues raise the hackles of distributors more than this one. Their reactions range from "grin and bear it" to outraged lawsuits or overt sabotage of the supplier's strategies. For example, Pennzoil, the parent company of Jiffy Lube International, the largest U.S. quick-lube franchiser, competes with Jiffy Lube via its own Pennzoil quick-lube shops. The result? The franchises at Jiffy Lube have brought suit against Pennzoil in court for hundreds of millions of dollars in alleged damage to their franchises.[11]

Federal Express is not only in the air express freight business but performs its own freight forwarding in the United States. When Federal Express bought Flying Tigers International in 1989, it did so to become a global player in air freight express shipping,[12] depending heavily on independent agents to handle freight-forwarding logistics for them in destinations across the Pacific. These agents, however, mindful that Federal Express does its own forwarding in the United States, are afraid Federal Express might eventually cut them out of the action in the future. These agents therefore often specify other carriers in their freight shipment arrangements in order to maintain business ties, despite the fact that many agents formerly specified Flying Tigers as preferred shippers prior to the Federal Express takeover.

Of course, manufacturers who integrate forward into reselling do not always find it a bed of roses. IBM sold its retail IBM Product Centers to Nynex when it discovered that its return on investment in retailing was far below its rate of return for its core manufacturing business.

The judgment call for a manufacturer almost always comes down to whether the company will reap more benefits (financial advantages, image control, knowledge of buying trends) from being in the distribution end of the business than it will forgo by alienating dealers whom it could otherwise enlist in the sale of its products.

Coca-Cola in Europe has opted to buy into its middlemen bottlers in the U.K., France, Germany, and Holland because it believes it needs distribution control to boost share with retailers.[13] Coke has invested $385 million to do so and has replaced the bottling managers with its own personnel. Coke feels it can implement more aggressive bottler pricing, delivery, and merchandising with retailers if its own people are in charge.

On the other hand, other companies such as Steelcase in office furniture have pledged never to compete with their dealers directly because they believe the costs and risks of such a strategy far outweigh the gains.

Novel Distribution Channels

Sometimes the marketing channels that provide gateway access to markets are plugged with competitive products, and a manufacturer cannot gain entry. In such a case the manufacturer may need to innovate and either set up a new channel or exploit one nobody else has thought about. Snap-on Tools faced such a situation when its mechanics' tools were refused by incumbent tool distributors, who already carried multiple brands. Snap-on set up a unique system of Snap-on Tools franchises that deliver, clean, finance, replace, and sell its tools right on site at the mechanic's place of work. When Avon initially couldn't sell its cosmetics via department stores (the usual route), it went door-to-door with part-time commissioned neighborhood-based Avon reps. When Hanes L'eggs pantyhose met a less than optimum reaction in discount and drug store chains, it innovated by selling in grocery stores, a unique method for marketing pantyhose at the time. Church's shoes markets its shoes in upscale men's apparel shops instead of shoe stores—a strategy that resulted in Church's selling 80,000 pairs of shoes throughout Europe in 1989.

If traditional channels are the only way to get to market, a company may choose to piggyback another company's distribution network and contacts. For example, Whirlpool sells its appliances in Japan through channels controlled by Sony, the electronics giant. Similarly, Warner-Lambert markets its Schick brand razors and blades in Japan through Seiko's controlled distribution.

There is clearly more than one way to skin a cat in establishing channel pathways to market.

Distribution Coverage and Cost Containment

While the focus on low-cost manufacturing is a competitive imperative in many industries, the distribution choices a company makes to cover its customers and markets also drive costs. A business that is astute at low-cost manufacturing but that chooses distribution coverage options without considering their cost impacts runs the risk of forfeiting any manufacturing cost advantages to competitors who use more cost-efficient distribution strategies. It may well be, for instance, that the personal computer maker with the most cost-efficient dealer network covering end customers will emerge the winner in the battle for market share, rather than the lowest cost maker of machines. That is why so much time, money, and attention are spent by Compaq, Apple, and IBM on dealer selection, recruitment, programming, training, motivating, and monitoring. In fact, unless attention is paid to cost-efficient dealer network design, companies will derive a much weaker payoff from other marketing spending areas such as advertising, public relations, or packaging, since product availability and display for customers are compromised by inadequate coverage.

Direct Sale

A company that decides as a matter of policy to sell end customers directly instead of using distributors faces a number of cost challenges.

Because distributors typically provide markets with rapid order turnaround even on small orders, a business faces higher order transaction costs when it sells direct to many small end users (compared to the cost of selling to distributors, who in turn fill smaller orders from their stock). In addition, carrying costs escalate since the number of accounts receivable increase. By interfacing directly with end users, the company loses the benefit of fewer but larger accounts receivable from large consolidated distributor orders; in addition, it may face higher average inventories and attendant carrying costs, because it must invest in multiple stocking locations in order to service end users in a timely manner. In an indirect sale mode, such multiple locations would belong to various distributors in each market. Selling costs also increase without distributors, since end user customers must be contacted in accordance with preferred buying cycles and the manufacturer is not sharing such account servicing activity with an appointed network of distributors. An organization selling through distribution often sends its sales force to end users only to generate increased demand, leaving fill-in order calls on customers to be handled by the distributor. This, of course, doesn't occur in direct sale.

Direct sales can often only be justified if products command sizeable gross margins, accounts can be manageably covered (not too many), and after-sale service revenue is also attractive.

Channel Variety

When a business opts to sell through a variety of distribution channels, it is faced with the costs of customizing its products, packaging, promotional supports, and advertising materials *by channel*—costs not faced by a business using a single channel to market its products.

Consider, for example, a full-line manufacturer of lightbulbs that may be sold in some or all of as many as a dozen different distribution channels, including department stores, mass merchants, grocery stores, hardware stores, home building supply stores, convenience stores, drug chains (or independents), specialty lighting stores, warehouse clubs, and decorating stores featuring bathroom or kitchen fixtures.

Whenever the lightbulb manufacturer expands the variety of distribution channels into which it sells, it faces the challenge of customizing its marketing. For instance, the assortment breadth offered is different in a drugstore than in a building supply store in terms of lightbulb sizes, amperages, colors, shapes, and number of multi-packs offered, because the drugstore's shelf and display space is so much more limited. The promotional supports for point of sale also vary, as do advertising programs, since the drug chain may use flyer promotions extensively while the building supply store uses newspaper ads. A warehouse club may require specialized bundling of only common popular-selling lightbulbs at rockbottom prices, drop-shipped to their locations, and require no advertising supports or point-of-sale materials. Specialty lighting stores may want upscale in-store planograms, including collateral ad materials about specialized kinds of light bulbs (energy savers, long-life bulbs, special shapes, bulbs for track lighting, and so forth).

Clearly, the policy decision to sell to highly varied channels carries considerable implications for market program/product customization costs. In the quest for growth, companies using single channels often expand market coverage by adding additional channels. For instance, New England Business Service, a $226 million manufacturer of business forms, decided to expand outside its narrow direct mail distribution channel. It added 10,000 business form printers and stationery shops in hopes of increasing sales to $1 billion. This initiative resulted in new cost challenges.

Channel Ownership

A company that decides to own or franchise its channels of distribution incurs a number of distinct costs. Owned channels, in which the business integrates forward to control the point of sale as a distributor or retailer, involves all of the attendant costs of such operations, including site financing and taxes, utilities, site maintenance, labor and benefit costs, inventories, machinery, supervision, data processing, and consumable supplies and other overheads.

Square D, an electrical manufacturer, is solidifying its distribution network in Europe prior to the institution of a unified market throughout the European Community in 1992 by assuming equity positions in key European electrical wholesalers. This will provide higher distributor control but increase Square D's costs in ways it has not faced before.

In a franchised operation the company either shares or avoids the costs of operating distribution channels through its relationship with its franchisees. Another alternative chosen by some manufacturers or service providers is to lease or rent facilities to control distribution; for example, cosmetics makers may lease counter and floor space inside a department store, in which case only some distribution costs (such as costs of displays, inventories, labor, and supervision) apply.

Choosing to sell through independent autonomous distributors or retailers is clearly the lowest-cost option, albeit an option that offers less control of market image and operation than is possible with owned or franchised channels.

Distributor or Retailer Density

A company's costs are greatly affected by decisions about how many distributors (or retailers) it will sell through in a given geographic area. Having a great many retailers or distributors in an area increases the cost of training, supervising, and monitoring; in fact, large, dense networks of dealers often strain the resources and capabilities of suppliers who must provide network supervision, training programs, regular performance reviews, and contract sign-ups. Selling through fewer distributors makes such tasks more manageable and less costly, especially if the more selective networks' sales equal approximately 80 percent of the sales that would have been achieved by setting up all possible dealers. For instance, WD-40 only gives its product line to dealers or distributors with multiple outlets or accounts; it will not set up everyone who wants its line.

Denser networks often increase logistic and transaction costs as well, because such networks include small-volume dealers who place small orders and who tend to live hand-to-mouth because of undercapitalization and limited managerial talent. Bad debts and higher credit costs are also more prevalent with dense dealer networks comprising a high percentage of marginally creditworthy accounts.

Any business contemplating the addition of distributors or retailers to its network should always weigh the impact of such a move on its costs. A number of Hollywood studios, for example, are cutting back their efforts to sell their videocassette movies through thousands of small, single-outlet video rental shops that are prone to bankruptcy and are putting more efforts into working with national chains such as Kmart, Wal-Mart, and Sears, who sold millions of copies of popular titles such as Disney's *Who Framed Roger Rabbit?* and Warner Brothers' *Batman*.

Understanding Roles—The Key to Successful Distribution

Getting marketing channels to work for a manufacturer or service provider requires that each understand the other's role in the marketing process. Manufacturers have primary responsibility for developing market demand; they must therefore focus on developing end-user applications for their products; on modifying, upgrading, and launching new products for emerging needs; and on ensuring their sales representatives have the technical expertise and product knowledge to interface successfully with end users. The distributor is responsible for servicing demand, adequately inventorying its suppliers offerings, delivering to end users on a responsive basis, and calling in the manufacturer's sales or technical staff when end users need answers to usage or technical questions that the distributor is unqualified to handle.

When both the manufacturer and distributor understand these roles, the channel system has a much better chance of working well. Relations will be much smoother if both partners exchange market information with each other freely and tolerate occasional lapses in performance to preserve the longer-term loyalty of the other. A manufacturer who does not remain competitive on both product quality and price so that its distributors can sell its line profitably should expect its distributors to switch to its rivals' lines. For its part, a distributor who does not make every effort to service "developed" business on behalf of a supplier should in turn expect to be replaced by a distributor who can be trusted to do the job better. Channel partnerships always work best when there is agreement on these "first principles."

Notes

1. Barbara Bell and Richard Brandt, "Apple: New Team, New Strategy," *Business Week* (October 15, 1990), pp. 92, 93.
2. Brian Dumaine, "The New Turnaround Champs," *Fortune* (July 16, 1990), p. 42.
3. William Marsano, "New England Buyways," *Destinations Magazine* (Spring 1989), pp. 9–11.
4. For a good discussion of this topic, see Frank W. Cespedes and E. Raymond Corey, "Managing Multiple Channels," *Business Horizons* (July–August 1990), pp. 67–77.
5. George Fodor, "Shared Data Fosters Quality," *Industrial Distribution* (July 1990), pp. 43–44.
6. Doug Harper, "Councils Launch Sales Ammo," *Industrial Distribution* (September 1990), p. 28.
7. "Rx for Dealer Turnover: Pay Them to Stay," *Sales & Marketing Management* (September 1990), p. 33.
8. Arthur Andersen & Company, *Facing the Forces of Change: Beyond Future Trends in Wholesale Distribution* (Washington, D.C.: Distribution Research and Education Foundation, 1987), pp. 32, 33.
9. John Bonnanzio, "The Urge to Merge," *Industrial Distribution* (July 1989), p. 35.

10. Claire Poole, "Quick Change Artist," *Forbes* (December 10, 1990), pp. 158–160.
11. William P. Barrett, "Another Rabbit Please," *Forbes* (December 10, 1990), pp. 92, 98.
12. Sandra L. Kirsch, "Federal Express's Battle Overseas," *Fortune* (December 3, 1990), pp. 137–140.
13. "Coca-Cola Buys Into Bottlers in Europe," *Fortune* (August 13, 1990), pp. 68–73.

4

Alliances and Collaborative Ventures

There is tremendous cost—and risk—in establishing your own distribution, logistics, manufacturing, sales, and research and development in every key market around the globe. . . . Globalization mandates alliances, makes them absolutely essential to strategy.

Kenichi Ohmae
"The Global Logic of Strategic Alliances"
Harvard Business Review
(March–April 1989)

Almost as important as meeting the inexorable pressure for enhanced marketing and staying innovative is the need for a company to partner with others for growth. There have always been several strategies to satisfy growth objectives, but, for better or worse, several of these have become riskier and more expensive than they were in the past. Figure 4-1 diagrams these common growth strategies.

Strategies for Growth

Establishing Foreign Subsidiaries

Many of the world's largest companies—industrial/commercial companies such as IBM, ICI, 3M, and Asea Brown Boveri and consumer-goods companies such as Procter & Gamble, Bata Shoe,

Figure 4-1. Common growth options of corporations.

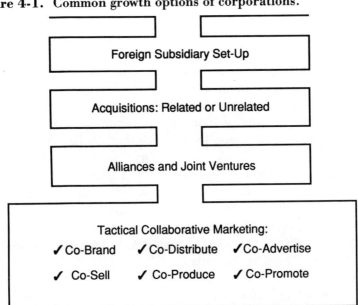

and Nestlé—have grown through the establishment of extensive foreign subsidiary operations. Each of these companies planted its roots early in foreign soil, allowing subsidiary operations to grow into sizable businesses in their own right. This strategy made a great deal of sense when market and technology changes were less dramatic and more evenly paced. The company could learn its way, investing nation by nation in market development activities, local manufacturing, and logistical self-sufficiency as the volume of sales grew. As nations' standards of living improved, the demand for IBM computers, Nestlé coffee, 3M tape, and Bata shoes frequently also rose, providing excellent returns on companies' investments and encouraging them to cede autonomy to their subsidiary companies in functions typically closely controlled by headquarters, such as acquisitions and research and development. In effect, they reinvested much of their profits back into the subs that had generated them in the first place. These businesses continue to pursue this strategy; they are establishing new subs to serve markets such as China, the Soviet Union, and the nations of Eastern Europe. In each of these geographic areas, long-term investments in freestanding subs will likely pay off, albeit over an extended time frame.

As the pace of market change quickens, businesses that have not yet established international subs must pursue other growth avenues. It is both time-consuming and costly to establish a sub in Europe in hopes of participating in the growing European economic harmonization. Companies don't have the luxury of time to prepare to capitalize on the opportunities afforded by the European preference to buy locally, nor do they have the financial resources necessary to do so. Setting up a subsidiary when money costs approach 20 percent is not likely to yield a high enough return to justify the investment. Japanese companies have more flexibility because their costs of capital are often in single digits. In addition, many Japanese companies are cash-rich and can therefore afford to grow according to the traditional multinational subsidiary setup formula.

Acquiring Existing Businesses

With the establishment of foreign subsidiary operations a financially risky and time-consuming game, many companies are looking at acquisitions as the way to grow geographically. Unfortunately, acquisition as a strategy often resembles the siren's song in Homer's *Odyssey*—seductive but fraught with unseen risks. In a study of more than 2,000 acquisitions made by thirty-three large companies between 1950 and 1980, Michael Porter of Harvard discovered that the results of the acquisitions were so below the buyers' expectations that half were divested (sold off or closed down) by 1986. Many of the problems with acquisitions boil down to unjustifiably high purchase prices, excessive debt taken on by the acquisitor to finance the buy, or the acquisitor's lack of familiarity with the purchased company's industry, making it hard to integrate the acquisition into the acquisitor's existing structure.

When McKinsey and Company studied a variety of acquisitions to determine the percentage success rate and the primary reasons for failure, it found that in only 23 percent of the acquisitions analyzed did management earn financial returns exceeding the cost of funds to secure the purchase. Key reasons for failure were management's propensity to overestimate the synergy that would result from adding the acquired company's line of business to its own; management's overestimation of the target acquisition's potential growth prospects; and management's underestimation of integration difficulties.

Consider the European Community—an inviting market to many outsiders who want a stake in the expansion expected to result from the 1992 economic unification. Acquisition looks like the surest way to gain access to this growing market while building on an existing base of volume and customers. Unfortunately, finding suitable acquisition candidates is anything but easy in Europe. Many of the potential target companies are privately held, with unique share structures. This means stock swaps aren't very practical, and cash becomes the method of purchase. Valuing the company is a tough exercise because accounting procedures vary from those accepted in the United States. Information sources on European targets are often incomplete, out of date, or not available at all; for instance, outside of France, Germany, Italy, and the United Kingdom, source standard references such as Dun and Bradstreet reports and 10-K security filings are simply not present. Finding a suitable acquisition target can be extremely difficult.

After the acquisition is complete, the purchaser is still left with the problems of integrating the acquisition into its own set-up, even assuming an astute financial preparation and "fit" analysis has been done. A survey of 200 chief executives showed that an acquiring company's ability to integrate its purchase was the telling success factor in making acquisition strategy work. These chief executives emphatically confessed disappointment with the abilities of their own companies to do this successfully.[1]

Consider the case of Bridgestone,[2] which acquired Firestone Tire and Rubber Company for $2.8 billion in 1988. Instead of a combined stronger performance, the two companies have seen their consolidated profits fall precipitously. Losses at Firestone have pulled overall profits from levels in excess of $250 million in 1988 to $67 million on sales of $11.9 billion in 1990. So severe have been the problems of integrating and streamlining Firestone and improving the productivity of its operations that Bridgestone has had to cut back its own U.S. expansion plans as well as dispatch

Japanese management from its head office to oversee the merger. Putting the companies together, it turns out, took two years longer than anticipated, and the effort has produced fewer efficiencies than were expected when the acquisition was made. Yet this acquisition had all the earmarks of success, since the two companies had synergy in their basic businesses, from their product mixes sold to their similar customers, distributors, emphasis on quality processes, operational productivity, and factory automation. It would seem that in the case of acquisitions not only does Murphy's Law operate but O'Brien's Law as well.

Murphy's Law states that if something can go wrong, it will—and at exactly the wrong time. In our example, shortly after Bridgestone acquired Firestone, a price war on tires broke out in Europe (where Firestone was strong); a civil war occurred in Liberia (where Firestone owns a large rubber plantation); Firestone lost its General Motors tire supply contract; and economic dislocation hit Latin America (another Firestone market share stronghold).

O'Brien's Law states that "Murphy was an optimist." In fact, Bridgestone discovered, when it saw its newly acquired company's operations up close that Firestone's factory productivity was far worse than it imagined (less than half of Bridgestone's). To make matters worse, because Firestone has now begun to lose money, it cannot write off interest expenses on the debt Bridgestone used to buy it (which had been placed on Firestone's balance sheet). It seems as if O'Brien was particularly astute in his view of Murphy!

This is not to say that an acquisition strategy cannot ever pay back. In Italy, the first, second, fourth, and fifth largest operating companies in express distribution have been acquired since 1987 and are being managed successfully by foreigners. Federal Express has made an acquisition strategy pay off for it by participating in some of these acquisitions.

Cooper Industries has successfully acquired 60 different companies mostly in the 1980s. Most of its acquisitions are not identified with the Cooper name, they include Champion Spark Plug, McGraw-Edison, Crouse-Hinds, Belden, and Cameron Iron Works.

One common problem with acquisitions is loss of focus. For

instance, Gerber, the baby-food maker, diversified by acquisition into furniture, trucking, stuffed toys, and truck farming, areas in which it had no expertise. It wound up selling off each of these subsidiaries in 1988 to refocus on its core baby-food product lines; the acquisitions had flopped in terms of helping Gerber grow profitably. Stanley Tools owes 50 percent of its $2 billion sales to acquisitions, and its success has been due to the focused fit of these companies to Stanley's core tool business.

Japanese companies in the 1990s are increasingly turning to acquisition as a strategy to establish "insider" status in large markets such as Europe and the United States. While Japanese companies spent $53 billion in 1989 to buy U.S. companies, U.S. businesses spent only $17 billion to purchase companies in Japan. Similarly, Japanese businesses spent $34 billion to buy European-based companies, while European businesses spent only $3 billion in Japan. The Japanese are attracted by market opportunity and can afford to spend so much because they have healthy balance sheets. *Fortune* and *Business Week* magazines reported that of the twenty-six companies worldwide with over $1 billion or more in cash on their balance sheets (net of debt) in 1988, nineteen were Japanese, including giants such as Matsushita, Toyota, Hitachi, Toshiba, Nippon Oil, Nissan Motor, Kirin Brewery, and Sanyo Electric.

Additional problems plaguing acquisition or merger strategies are similar in kind and degree to those plaguing efforts to start subsidiaries from scratch. Finding the right candidate and integrating it can take two to five years, too much time to take advantage of emerging markets such as that in Europe or to compete successfully in high-tech fast-paced fields where technology becomes obsolete in less time than the acquisition process consumes. Two to five years in the computer industry could represent two to five new generations of product technology.

Forming Alliances and Joint Ventures

While the management of an alliance or joint venture is just as complex and difficult as managing an acquisition, strengthening market position through a cooperative venture does have distinct advantages. Alliances can be consummated quickly—a big plus in a fast-paced world. When windows of market opportunity close quickly, cooperative ventures allow a business to leapfrog into a growing yet fleeting market successfully.

For instance, Sony has undertaken a variety of alliances with domestic U.S. corporations to get a jump in new technologies. It has an alliance with Panavision, Inc., of Tarzana, California, to develop jointly a lens for high-definition television. It has an alliance with Exabyte of Boulder, Colorado, to develop 8mm tapes that will be compatible with Exabyte's Computer Storage systems. Sony also has an alliance with Compression Labs, Inc., of San Jose, California, to develop a video-conferencing machine. In each case Sony contributes staff resources, production facilities, and business planning assistance to the alliance instead of taking an equity partner position.

Cooperative ventures often cost less to operate or enter into than do start-ups or acquisitions; they can often be consummated in several markets for the cost of only one acquisition (AT&T found this to be the case in Europe as it established alliances with Philips, Olivetti, and Italatel). If a joint venture fails, it usually costs far less than a failed acquisition. Arco joint ventured with Ericsson of Sweden to try to diversify from oil and gas into office markets. When this venture collapsed, both companies' losses were so minor the press did not even report them.[3] Yet when Exxon similarly tried to diversify from the oil business into office products but did so by acquisition, its losses exceeded $1 billion before the effort was abandoned.

Alliances and joint ventures can be very flexible since managements from both companies can handpick those they wish to champion and run the allied operation; in the case of acquisitions, severe morale problems can emerge when or if new management is put in to run or integrate the acquired company (or to achieve cost savings from cutting overhead).

Alliances can allow companies to achieve vertical integration, as IBM has done with Intel in the supply of computer chips for IBM equipment componentry. In addition, an alliance can help a company overcome legal or regulatory barriers, since the alliance partner may be in a position to assist with otherwise unobtainable market access.

An alliance or joint venture can provide a highly effective

competitive position in an industry. For instance, Airbus, the aerospace consortium of German, British, French, and Spanish partners, is now Boeing's biggest global competitor in aircraft manufacturing. Last year, Airbus sold 350 large aircraft worldwide. GE's joint venture with France's SNECMA to build aircraft engines has given it a very strong position both in European commercial markets and with military customers on both sides of the Atlantic.

Alliances allow companies to gain access to new technologies they often need to complete their own product offerings but which are too expensive or problematical to fund. For instance, a computer company needs software to sell hardware. But developing leading-edge computer hardware is an expensive venture in its own right, without the added cost of trying to be state-of-the-art in all sorts of software. Alliances between IBM or DEC and software companies such as Microsoft or Lotus allow each to benefit;[4] the large company acts as a credible reference for the smaller software maker's products, while the large business helps to bring software to market that increases the productivity of its own computers and expands the attractiveness of hardware to solve more customer problems, thus expanding the total market for system solutions.

As technologies overlap, alliances become even more important. For instance, in the past, pharmaceutical companies did not have to be experts in genetics to develop and produce drugs. Today, breakthroughs in DNA research allow biotechnology companies such as Genentech to develop products such as genetically engineered human insulin. Companies such as Eli Lilly, which markets Genentech's insulin, have had to ally themselves with cutting-edge research companies to keep pace with technologies that displace their own.

In a similar vein, companies such as DuPont, Celanese, and Hercules are producing new materials and polymers that outperform traditional products such as steel and aluminum. Unless the makers of traditional steel and aluminum ally themselves with companies producing the newer materials, they will find they cannot compete on orders for lighter-weight, more energy-efficient car and aircraft bodies and parts.

Joint ventures can be very profitable; Corning's joint ventures produce more than half of its profits. Corning has stretched its own capacity through its joint ventures by adding a partner's competence to that of its own. Corning's expertise in spun glass was combined with Owen-Illinois in 1938 to produce fiberglass insulation in the Owens-Corning joint venture. Its discovery of silicon, made from silica and plastic, allowed it to form an alliance (Dow-Corning) to exploit uses for silicon. Corning's substantial ownership of these two companies today produces a steady stream of dividend income. In fact, had Thomas Edison not worked jointly with Corning in the early 1900s, lightbulbs could not have been made at a low enough cost to become the mass success they became. Corning invented the ribbon machine, in which a ribbon of hot glass can be shaped using compressed air to form lightbulbs at a rate of 2,000 bulbs a minute. Corning's joint venture in Europe with CIBA-Geigy to produce medical/ diagnostic products has been extremely successful.

Fuji-Xerox,[5] a joint venture between Rank Xerox and Fuji Film, has become a $3 billion-plus-a-year operation earning very good profits in Japan. Hewlett-Packard's joint venture with Yoko-gawa Electric of Japan earns 5½ percent net profit after tax and has grown since 1963 into a $750 million Japanese-based operation.

Alliances can assist a company in balancing its sales geo-graphically. Hewlett-Packard has a much more geographically balanced sales mix globally than all its European rivals; Siemens sells 85 percent of its computers in Europe, and Olivetti of Italy and Bull of France have computer sales heavily concentrated in their home country markets. Hewlett-Packard has engineered a string of alliances so that now more than 50 percent of its sales are outside North America. Figure 4-2 lists some of the many alliances Hewlett-Packard has entered into in order to balance its worldwide business geographically.[6]

Alliances can represent the only acceptable foreign entry vehicle into some nations. For example, in the countries of East-ern Europe, such arrangements meet the economic and political goals of the governments. The Marriott, Hilton, Sheraton, and Hyatt International Corporation have each opened joint venture hotels in cities such as Warsaw, Poland; Budapest, Hungary; Sofia, Bulgaria; and Belgrade, Yugoslavia. While getting its profits

Figure 4-2. Hewlett-Packard's alliances: a partial listing (August 1989).

Product Alliance	Partner
High-Powered, Low-Cost Computer Workstations	Samsung (Korea)
Precision Architecture Computer Chip Technology	Hitachi (Japan)
"Brainy" Typewriters and Printers	Canon (Japan)
Logic Systems	Yokogawa (Japan)
Microprocessor Development Systems	Northern Telecom (Canada)
Digital Audio Tapes	Sony (Japan)
Management Consulting on Computer Integrated Manufacturing (CIM)	Arthur Andersen (U.S.)
Printed Circuit Board Manufacturing in Puerto Rico	Oki Electric (Japan)

out of the country as hard currency is a problem, each chain has had no problems fully renting rooms in these accommodation-starved locations, where few local competitors can match the chains' service expertise and reservation and accounting systems.[7]

Obtaining hard currency or saleable goods in exchange for products or services can be a real challenge in some nations. Siemens' agreement with the government of Bulgaria to supply digital switches may require it to accept wood or agricultural products in exchange for the switches the joint venture will produce and sell.

Political instability can make it difficult to negotiate joint ventures because it can be very hard to find the right person to sign a valid contract or joint venture deal. As Eastern Europe moves to a market economy, persons holding positions of authority are changing quickly. Motorola found this to be the case when it tried to establish a venture for producing cellular telephones with a partner in Hungary.

One of the key issues in forming alliances is sorting out the measurements to use when evaluating their desirability. The motives for entering into them can be *market-based* (gaining access, helping preempt rivals, or gaining distribution); *technological* (integrating production or developing new products jointly); or *legal* or *regulatory* (overcoming a legal barrier to entry). Measurements of success or failure must be matched to motives; the assessment of alliances cannot use only financial criteria to measure results. Achieving scale economies, higher R.O.I., asset utilization, or profit returns is only one of many possible measures of success. Clearly, market or technology measures, including market share/competitive position, penetration of target markets, cycle time required to develop new products or exploit joint technologies, or conversion of the market to new alliance-produced products, could also be used.

Joint Venture Trend Data

While some large companies have engaged in well-publicized alliances and joint ventures, in fact joint venturing as a trend is widespread. Kathryn Harrigan's pathbreaking books[8] catalog the extent of this activity. As Figure 4-3 shows, joint venturing varies considerably by industry, with low participation rates in industries such as software and high participation rates (more than 25 percent) in pharmaceuticals and computers. The trend in every case, however, demonstrates considerable increases in joint venturing activity. For instance, in automobile manufacture and assembly, joint venturing between companies is extensive, including deals between Ford and Mazda, Toyota and GM, and Chrysler and Mitsubishi. In industries such as oil, gas, mining, and insurance, joint ventures allow for risk sharing in mega-projects that would be beyond the means of one company to undertake. For instance, when GE and France's state-owned SNECMA linked up in a joint venture to produce a low-pollution engine for high-performance aircraft, they did so because the $800 million expense of the project exceeded the amount each company was willing to spend on a go-it-alone basis but was acceptable when shared.[9]

Joint venturing was formerly used to gain market access in

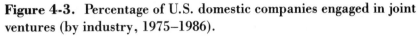

Figure 4-3. Percentage of U.S. domestic companies engaged in joint ventures (by industry, 1975–1986).

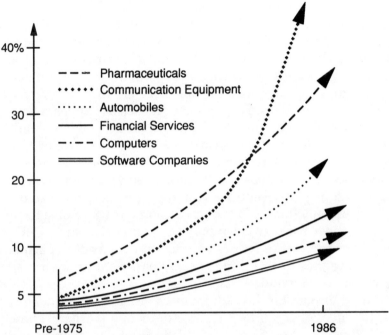

Source: Adapted from Kathryn R. Harrigan, "Joint Ventures and Competitive Strategies," *Strategic Management Journal*, Vol. 9 (1988), pp. 144, 145.

Third World countries or to distribute products to a market that would otherwise be unreachable. Today, joint venturing is much more strategic. It is undertaken as an integral part of a global strategy allowing companies to pool complementary resources and skills and to conquer market share in less time with less cost and risk than they would face going it alone or trying the acquisition route. That is why alliances between competitors such as IBM and Apple are taking place despite long-standing marketplace rivalries.

The Pitfalls of Joint Ventures

While the trend to more joint ventures is clear, alliances are neither risk free nor a guarantee of success. Alliances can be an expedient, but they often cannot be relied upon totally to provide sustainable competitive advantages. Alliances can be used to paper over a company's strategic weaknesses, but when a recession hits and competition heat up, such weaknesses often surface despite the alliance. Unfortunately, if a recession hits one venture partner harder than the other, the weaker partner can find itself at the mercy of the stronger coalition partner.

The most problem-plagued alliances are fifty-fifty ventures, which are often the most popular. The reason appears to be a breakdown in communication and decision making resulting from the fact that neither partner has clearcut control or leadership. AT&T's collapsed venture with Olivetti in the marketing and manufacture of personal computers suffered from this problem. When fifty-fifty ventures run into problems, often they can be resolved only if the CEOs of each company agree on a formula to solve the particular dilemma. Unfortunately, such CEO involvement often takes far too long to happen, as each partner in the venture tries to sort things out by passing it up their respective chain of command.

Another pitfall in fifty-fifty joint ventures is their inability to adapt as market conditions change or as one partner's strategic focus changes. Dow Chemical and BASF of Germany formed a fifty-fifty joint venture that fell apart when BASF wanted to expand it and Dow did not. BASF eventually wound up buying out Dow's shares and running the business as a separate wholly-owned company.

Joint ventures between companies from different cultures can be particularly fragile because of communication problems inherent in different languages and value systems. Japanese companies are often reluctant to form joint ventures with U.S. businesses because the latter replace their senior managements more often, while the Japanese place great value on trust and continuity in personal managerial relationships to make such ventures work in the long run. The Japanese believe turnover at the top signals lowered commitment to the venture. Similarly, Pirelli and Dunlop were unable to develop a workable Anglo-Italian culture in their joint venture tire alliance, and the venture collapsed in 1981.

Inconsistencies between two alliance partners' accounting systems and information systems can also present formidable obstacles to smooth working arrangements. If accounting issues can't be ironed out, problems in cost allocations, timing of purchases, depreciation formulas, and pricing—all vitally important if the partners are to reconcile operating results—will surface.

Rules for Completing Successful Alliances

Quite apart from the need to seek a partner with a compatible culture and management values* and synergistic operating systems, following some general rules of thumb can raise the prospects of success in a joint venture. They include:

• *Seek partners where some measure of mutual dependence is present.* This practice ensures that each has a vested interest in seeing its own needs and expectations met by keeping the joint venture working. Both partners should have a medium level of dependence on the skills or capabilities of the other. If there is too little dependence, the venture will collapse in tough times; too much mutual dependence leads to insecurity and hedging of trust, with each partner overly concerned about the loss of the other.

• *Clarify the venture's mission in concrete terms.* This step includes not merely the timing and level of financial returns expected but the goals desired in terms of results in the market, such as market share or the strategic position the venture wants to attain in the industry. Unless objectives are clarified up front and go beyond financial reasons, the venture will likely flounder. Ambiguity in a mission leads to indecisiveness; partnerships entered into strictly for financial reasons often don't last over the long haul since volatile returns plague almost any new venture, especially those set up to exploit new markets or technologies. A clear mission also helps partners understand the limits of the collaboration. Joint venture agreements often fail when collaborators become competitors in other markets; by spelling out expectations, the partners make the nature of the collaboration

---

*For instance, U.S. executives often equate management with power and control, while the Japanese and Europeans believe management is all about collaboration and consensus.

explicit, and each partner understands at the outset how and where it may collide with its ally in other markets. It can then decide if it can trust the partner in any arrangements involving technology transfer or access to specialized resources (trade secrets or exceptionally talented individuals). A number of U.S.-Japanese joint ventures have failed when the Japanese partners took advantage of U.S. technology transfers and turned around to compete directly with their partners. This occurred in the office equipment market with the Canon–Bell and Howell partnership and the Ricoh—Savin alliance. There is always the risk with competitor alliances that the competitor is using a Trojan horse strategy—that is, one alliance partner wants access to the other's technology and markets; once it's got them, it cuts its alliance partner adrift. The other partner can then wind up with a brand-new competitor—its former partner, newly trained by it.

Collaborations with partners who compete in other markets can work. For instance, PPG and Asahi Glass are fierce competitors in sheet glass markets but have two joint-venture-managed factories producing automotive glass in America.

• *Involve top management.* Their participation confers legitimacy on the venture and helps break deadlocks that occur between the partners' operating level managers. Top management involvement also guarantees that top talent will be assigned to the venture to give it the best possible chance for success. International Computers Limited[10] tells its managers to treat all alliances as personal commitments because it believes that ultimately people make partnerships work (versus signed agreements, shared facilities, or joint equity arrangements).

• *Seek partners with complementary skills or resources.* One company might supply technology, and the other marketing coverage and manufacturing assets. For instance, in a new joint venture between DuPont and Merck, joint sales of the new company will be $700 million, with DuPont contributing 1,500 skilled researchers and $230 million as a first-year research and development budget; while the larger Merck will provide its research and development expertise, substantial cash, sales representation with doctors, and several promising new drugs.[11] In its joint venture with Indalsa of Spain, Atlantic Richfield (ARCO) contributes operating skills and a franchise system, plus one-third of the equity, while Indalsa contributes two-thirds of start-up equity to open, operate, and franchise 600 AM-PM minimarkets in Spain and Portugal.[12]

• *Develop plans early*. That way, financial forecasts, milestones, and objectives are agreed upon well in advance. In addition, the plans ought to spell out key success factors requiring mastery, an analysis of competitors, defined product specs, and all the necessary plans that relate to engineering, manufacturing, marketing, selling, and logistics. Putting plans in place enables the steering committee overseeing the venture to review results on a frequent basis as decisions move forward. Plans force partners to answer, early in the venture, questions such as:

—Will the market be there in future, and will it grow so we can grow?

—Will competitors knock out our technologies?

—Will gross margins be sustainable if there is a price war?

—Could a key resource bottleneck kill the venture's prospects?

• *Clarify the "unwind" provisions* should the venture result in a divorce. Determine how shares are to be disposed of; for instance, can partners buy out each other's share? A divorce clause should always be included in any joint venture arrangement.

• *Pick the right people to staff the venture,* and then provide them with autonomy to operate and the resources to get the job done. Good plans and clear goals are useless without talented people to head up any collaboration. Talented people will find ways to deal with changes that affect the venture, even when such changes are quite unpredictable at the time the venture begins.

• *Learn to share control,* since an alliance by its very nature involves ceding independence. This can be accomplished most easily by getting to know your partners *socially* at all levels. Friends find it easier to trust one another and are much less willing to fall out at the first sign of joint venture problems. Friends also are less likely to let red tape bog down important decisions. In the final analysis, there must be a central authority who can commit both partners to a clear course of action without resentment.

Types of Collaborative Ventures

Tactical Collaborative Ventures

Collaboration between companies need not always be strategic in the sense of setting up an entirely separate joint venture company. Businesses can undertake alliances in which the coalition involves only one part of the marketing mix.

Figure 4-4 diagrams the dimensions along which coalitions can be struck. As the figure shows, these dimensions can involve elements of the product's design, delivery, sale, promotion, packaging, pricing, or advertising.

By their nature, such collaborations are short-term and tactical rather than long-term and strategic. Nonetheless they can represent valuable methods for increasing a company's business. In a typical tactical venture, customers who bought goods worth more than $100 from a Tandy Radio Shack store received coupons valued up to $70 toward American Airline tickets. This boosted the business of both companies during the months the collaboration ran.

Product or Service Offering Alliances

A coalition between two companies can range in complexity along a continuum from straight licensed manufacture to joint manufacture of products that are mutually compatible in use to joint team design and production of the product.

In the least complex of these arrangements, a company can simply license its product formulation to another company for sale in the other's market. This is very common in pharmaceutical markets and between breweries. For instance, in Canada, most American and Australian beers are produced under license for sale in Canada under the licensor's brand name by either Labatts or Molsons, Canada's largest brewers.

Licensing in some industries has become a giant business.

Figure 4-4. Collaborative tactical alliances: dimensions for coalitions.

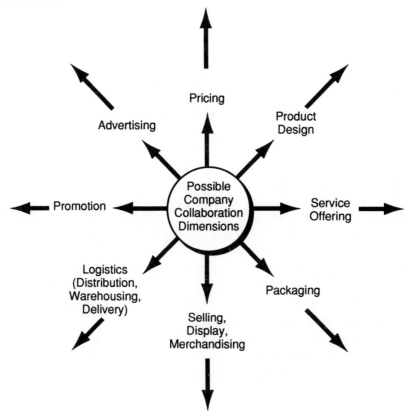

For instance, licensed apparel sales, which totalled $10 billion in 1980 in the United States, increased to more than $64 billion annually by 1989.

In the next level of complexity, a company may collaborate with another to ensure that its products are compatible in joint use by common customers. For instance, Apple Computer and Digital Equipment Corporation (DEC) set up such an alliance in 1988. DEC won the hearts of management information systems (MIS) departments with its VAX minicomputers. Apple, meanwhile, found its market among new personal computer users. Since computers today must share information, DEC and Apple have teamed up to guarantee that DEC's VAX machines and net/

OSI networks can work in a network with Apple's Macintosh desktops and "Apple Talk" networks. Any information run into a VAX can now wind up on a Macintosh, and vice versa; Macintosh users can share files and printers with VAX systems or retrieve information stored in a VAX system database. All of this is possible via Digital Equipment's LAN WORKS software and SQL/Services, offspring products from the collaborative product alliance.

Yet a third type of product alliance, the most complex, involves partners in the total design and manufacture of the product. Mazda and Ford, for example, have jointly engineered the new Ford Escort, which is produced in Ford and Mazda plants around the world. It is sold by Ford with the Escort name and under an alternate name by Mazda. Similarly, Ford's Louisville factory produces the Explorer, a utility vehicle of such high quality that Mazda makes a few cosmetic changes to the Explorer and sells it as a Mazda Navajos in its showrooms. This is the reverse of many Japanese-U.S. car company collaborations, in which traditionally the Japanese build the car and the U.S. dealers sell it under their brand name. (This is the case with Chrysler's Dodge Colt, built by Mitsubishi.)

Product collaborations need not involve companies making like products in the same industry, as with Ford and Mazda. For instance, Circle Fine Art of Chicago, which operates art galleries and distributes art to other galleries, and Bulova Corporation, which makes watches, have formed a joint venture company called Classic Moments Company. Classic Moments sells watches and clocks made by Bulova (priced between $32.50 and $250 wholesale) whose dials or faces feature reproductions of classic works of art by Van Gogh and Norman Rockwell, reproduced by artists under contract to Circle Fine Art. The watches are sold in art galleries, museums, and small gift shops, rather than in department stores or specialty chains. In 1989 this product collaboration sold $3.1 million in wholesale sales, and the collaboration will open dedicated stores to sell Classic Moments products.

Collaborations can also span services. For example, Kmart is collaborating with Little Caesar's to offer pizza in several Kmart stores in Michigan and Georgia, and Sears is negotiating with Kentucky Fried Chicken to test-market 1,400-square-foot Kentucky Fried Chicken complete-menu restaurants inside Sears stores. This type of collaboration allows each company to cash in on the store traffic generated by the other's consumer pull. Kentucky Fried Chicken or Little Caesar's would gain sales from Sears or Kmart shoppers while the retailers attract shoppers they might not otherwise gain or entice shoppers to remain in the store longer (and possibly continue to shop) because of the presence of these leading restaurant chains.

Each of the two retail chains believes such collaborations are also consistent with their attempts to include more brand names in their merchandise assortments. Little Caesar's and Kentucky Fried Chicken are brands with high recognition and associations with quality,[13] and this fits the Sears and Kmart "branded merchandise" emphasis perfectly.

Packaging, Display, and Sales Collaborations

While collaborations on products and services represent the most fundamental of market-mix partnerships since what is purchased is affected, a great many businesses also participate in packaging, display, or selling coalitions.

For example, the William Wrigley, Jr., Company has sold bubble gum in miniature look-alike pizza boxes licensed from Domino's Pizza and marketed through Wrigley's Amurol subsidiary, which merchandises children's gums and novelty candies.

Pizza Hut has teamed up with the producers of the Teenage Mutant Ninja Turtle videocassette series to include, inside the cassette package, Pizza Hut dinner coupons. This joint pack-up allows Pizza Hut to distribute its coupons to 8 million U.S. households, while the videocassette producers gain a value-added benefit for their package.

Display, merchandising, or selling alliances are also very valuable. For instance, many upscale restaurants in the Los Angeles area display works of art from local galleries. The paintings and works of art enhance the dining ambience while assisting galleries to gain exposure and sales leads.[14]

A good example of a merchandising and selling arrangement is that of Life Savers, Inc., marketers of Life Savers candy, Carefree sugarless gum, Bubble Yum, and Breath Savers. Life Savers looked around for an alliance that would leverage its superior retail merchandising skills, its national sales force, and its management depth in managing low-dollar-value confectionary products. It formed a coalition with Revlon's Norcliffe Thayer subsidiary to sell and merchandise single rolls of TUMS, the antacid tablet brand of Norcliffe. TUMS had strong existing distribution in drugstores and drug departments of discount stores, but the new alliance with Life Savers gave TUMS new growth in the confectionary departments of food chains, variety stores, and convenience chains.[15]

Selling alliances are frequently formed because one partner needs the sales coverage provided by the other. For example, Nestlé has a selling collaboration with General Mills to help General Mills improve sales of its Cheerios brand outside North America,[16] and Colgate-Palmolive has acted as selling partner for Wilkinson Blades in a great many markets over the years. It is very common for companies wishing to sell in Japan to collaborate with a company that is resident there and that has excellent distribution. For example, K. Hattori, which markets Seiko watches in Japan, also sells on behalf of Schick.

Logistics Alliances

Logistics alliances have mushroomed as computer technology has proliferated, the push to prune suppliers has grown stronger, and management's desire to "stick to its knitting" has caused companies to turn to external specialists where their own organizational logistics expertise is limited.

For example, Federal Express now fulfills Sharp's entire warehousing needs system in the United States. Federal Express guarantees to Sharp that it will deliver anywhere in the United States before 10:30 A.M. any order placed before 7 P.M. the previous day.[17] Sears Business Systems has a logistics alliance with Itel Distribution Systems of Alsip, Illinois, in which Itel modifies Sears equipment for special customer orders. Itel accomplishes this via its information system hook-up with Sears.

3M has an alliance with Abbott Laboratories to allow Abbott to warehouse and deliver all of 3M's medical and surgical products to hospital buyers across the United States. So successful has this alliance been that Abbott now also acts as the logistical supplier for Kimberly-Clark on nonwoven disposable products, C. R. Bard on urological products, Standard Register on business forms, and IBM on computer network services. To make logistics collaborations work, companies—especially manufacturers who shopped for the lowest bid prices from shippers or warehouses—must suspend their usual adversarial dealings.[18]

Collaborative Promotion or Advertising Programs

There are few areas of the market mix in which coalitions demonstrate as much creativity as in sales promotion and advertising. There are three basic types of coalitions that are used in sales promotion; these are shown in Figure 4-5.

1. *Two products are promoted together.* For example, Hanover Shoe of Hanover, Pennsylvania, co-promoted its Sportech Walking Shoes for the forty-five-year-old-and-up age group together with Mentholatum Co., makers of Deep-Heating Rub. A Hanover Shoe customer could buy the shoes for $19.99 (a special price) with a Mentholatum proof-of-purchase from Deep-Heating Rub.[19]

2. *A product and a service are promoted together.* For instance, Procter & Gamble cross-promoted Pepto-Bismol, its brand of stomach upset remedy, with H&R Block's tax preparation service,

Figure 4-5. Co-promotion possibilities between businesses.

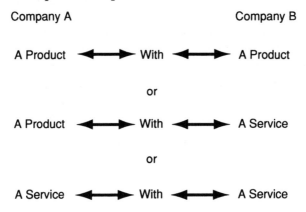

using the theme that each product helps reduce the stress of preparing one's own income tax return.[20]

3. *Two services are promoted together*. For example, McDonald's promotes itself through Sears, which is also in the service business. A considerable amount of service-and-service promotion is occurring between restaurants and oil company service stations; the gas stations distribute coupons for the restaurants to customers who fill their tank.

In some co-promotional collaborations, three companies get involved. For example, Revlon, the cosmetics maker, teamed up with Albertson's Department Stores and Merry Maids, a home cleaning service, to offer "Maid-for-a-Month" gift prizes to Albertson's customers who bought Revlon products through a special drawing. Albertson's and Revlon paid to advertise jointly the co-promotion in Sunday newspapers and in-store displays.

The more complex and innovative a co-promotion, the more it can provide an edge over a competitor. During the intense rivalry between Fuji and Kodak for market share in photographic film, Kodak formed an alliance with Timex, the watch manufacturer. Timex agreed to custom-manufacture a watch for $29.95 for any consumer using a Kodak photo negative as the watch face.[21] Such a creative promotion helped differentiate Kodak film from Fuji's. In a similar fashion, Procter & Gamble, waging a fierce market share war with Kimberly-Clark in disposable diapers, co-promotes with Rubbermaid's Little Tyke toy division; proofs-of-purchase for Luv's brand diapers are redeemed by Procter & Gamble for "checks" good for Little Tyke toy purchases.

Some co-promotion efforts involve extensive advertising campaigns. For instance, Pathe Entertainment (a movie studio) and the publisher Bantam Books co-promoted the movie and book *The Russia House*. Bantam promoted the movie with full-color inserts stuffed in each copy of the book, while Pathe produced a television ad to promote the movie and the book. On top of all of this, Bantam and Pathe produced ad materials to promote jointly the book and movie for magazines, newspapers, bookstores, and theaters. Such an elaborate co-promotion was consummated because consumers who read novels are much more likely to go to see the movie version of the book than are the general public (to Pathe's advantage). In addition, heavy advertising of any author's work later turned into a film has been proven to increase other book title sales by the same author (to Bantam's advantage).[22]

Pricing Coalitions

Companies can cross-connect in pricing arrangements, though this tactic is less frequently used than other tactical partnerships. Airlines, hotels, and car rental outfits have for many years arranged pricing to provide discounts on one another's services to frequent users.

One of the more unique pricing alliances attempted in recent years has been between retailers and credit card companies. In a nationwide pricing alliance, Kmart, Toys "R" Us, Montgomery Ward, Casual Corner, Sam Goody, and B. Dalton Booksellers, all large successful chain stores, hooked up with MasterCard on a price collaboration called Master Values. Shoppers at these stores received special price discounts on selected merchandise as long as it was purchased during the special Christmas pricing period (September to December). Store shoppers were informed of the pricing discounts and the merchandise each discount applied to via special discount books provided by each retailer or mailed with monthly MasterCard billing statements. The discount books contained redeemable coupons available for use at checkouts when the items were paid for with MasterCard. Items covered included jewelry, furniture, Mattel toys, clothing, and thousands of other items. This pricing alliance involved MasterCard and more than 5,000 retail outlets.[23]

Pricing partnerships of this sort allow for a three-way cost-risk sharing arrangement. MasterCard picked up some of the costs, as did the retailers and the brand-name suppliers whose merchandise was featured as part of the retailer's special promotional pricing. It is a win-win-win-win outcome, with the customers, the credit card company, the retailer, and the manufacturer all benefitting from the coalition of the two principal pricing partners.

Notes

1. Mark Daniell, "Webs We Weave," *Management Today* (U.K.) (February 1990), p. 82. Also see J. F. Weston, "The Payoff in Mergers and Acquisitions," in I. Rock and L. Milton, eds., *The Mergers and Acquisitions Handbook* (New York: McGraw-Hill, 1987).
2. Z. Schiller and R. Schreffler, "So Far, America Is a Blowout for Bridgestone," *Business Week* (August 6, 1990), pp. 82–83.
3. R. D. Lynch, "Building Alliances to Penetrate European Markets," *Journal of Business Strategy* (March–April 1990), pp. 4–8.
4. Peter Drucker, "The Futures That Have Happened Already," *The Economist* (December 15, 1989), p. 8.
5. Kenichi Ohmae, "The Global Logic of Strategic Alliances," *Harvard Business Review* (March–April 1989), pp. 149, 150.
6. "Safety in Numbers," *The Economist* (August 12, 1989), p. 57.
7. S. Pesmen, "U.S. Hotels Invade Eastern Europe on Strength of Their Service and Reputations," *Business Marketing* (October 1990), pp. 46–47.
8. Kathryn Harrigan, *Strategies for Joint Ventures* and *Managing for Joint Venture Success* (Lexington, Mass.: Lexington Books, 1986).
9. Howard Perlmutter and David Heenan, "Cooperate to Compete Globally," *Harvard Business Review* (March–April 1986), p. 136.
10. ———, "ICL's Do's for Successful Collaboration," *Harvard Business Review* (March–April 1986), p. 149.
11. Mike O'Neal, "DuPont and Merck a Tough New Duo?," *Business Week* (August 6, 1990), p. 38.
12. Nadia Pryszlak, "U.S. Companies International Joint Ventures," *Directors and Boards* (Spring 1990), p. 55.
13. "Castleguard, Inc., to Test Market Kentucky Fried Chicken in Sears," *Nation's Restaurants* (April 9, 1990), p. 4.
14. "Upscale Restaurants Display Artists' Work," *The Wall Street Journal* (April 23, 1987), p. 35.
15. George S. Day, *Market-Driven Management* (New York: The Free Press, 1990), p. 309.

16. John Marcom, Jr., "Feed the World," *Forbes* (October 1, 1990), p. 114.
17. *The Industrial Marketing and Research Association of Canada Newsletter*, Vol. 13, No. 9 (July 1990), p. 1.
18. Donald J. Bowersox, "The Strategic Benefits of Logistics Alliances," *Harvard Business Review* (July–August 1990), p. 44.
19. Bill Keenan, Jr., "What Do Award Winners Have in Common?" *Sales & Marketing Management* (January 1989), p. 72.
20. Allan J. Magrath, *"Market Smarts"* (New York: John Wiley & Sons, 1988), p. 29.
21. "Timex and Kodak Will Put You on the Face of Your Watch," *U.S.A. Today* (April 19, 1988), p. 4B.
22. "Pathe and Bantam Link Up to Promote Russia House," *Ad Week* (August 20, 1990), p. 4.
23. "Retailers and MasterCard Join Forces With Master Values," *Discount Store News* (August 6, 1990), p. 2.

5

The Globalization of Marketing

In marketing terms, I see true globalization as a commitment to viewing the world as a single market and focusing on maximum standardization of products. That means believing you can sell the same products in Tulsa, Tunisia or Timbuktu with equal success.

Preston Townley, "Global Business in the Next Decade"
Across the Board
January–February 1990

Today, it's easy to think of numerous products and services that are probably equally saleable in Tulsa, Tunisia, and Timbuktu—a Sony Walkman, a pair of Levi jeans, a Nestlé chocolate bar, an IBM personal computer, a bottle of Coca-Cola, an American Express credit card, a Mickey Mouse stuffed toy, a Gillette razor, a Xerox copier, a pair of Nike jogging shoes, a Toyota Corolla. In industry after industry, being a major league player means playing in the global marketplace. In industries such as the oil or chemical industry, where large-scale production is key, this has been the case for decades. But industries in which domestic players succeeding in home markets could ignore global prospects or competitors—the food industry, electronics industry, telecommunications industry, and automotive industry—are rapidly disappearing. Ford used to agonize about GM and Chrysler; today it worries as much about Honda, Toyota, and Nissan. While Honda is only two-thirds Chrysler's size in dollar sales, its 1989 profits were almost double Chrysler's. Similarly, Boeing used to concentrate only on McDonnell Douglas and Lockheed; now it must keep a close eye on Airbus Industries of Europe. GE always kept tabs on Westinghouse but now also monitors the likes of Siemens of Germany, Matsushita Electric of Japan, Thomson CSF of France, and Samsung of Korea.

Even in service businesses such as banking, advertising, publishing, retailing, food service, hotels, stock brokerage, and information services, the global players are the ones moving ahead fastest. And being huge in the United States doesn't mean you will dominate globally—in either sales or profit ranking. For example, in banking, Citicorp's assets totalled $230 billion in 1989, making it the largest bank in the United States. Yet there were five banks in Japan in 1989 with more than $300 billion in assets. While the U.S.-based Marriott hotel chain did $7.5 billion in 1979 sales, Britain's Trusthouse Forte made $341 million in profit on sales of $5 billion, compared to only $181 million in profit in that same year for Marriott.

Business Week magazine refers to these companies as "stateless corporations,"[1] since they seek to dominate markets globally by flowing their people, capital, and technologies in global directions based upon strategic opportunities for share and competitive one-upmanship. Owing allegiance to no particular market, companies such as IBM, McDonald's, Citicorp, Nestlé, Gillette, Dow Chemical, Hewlett-Packard, Honda, Seiko, Canon, Bayer, and Reuters sell the majority of their volume outside their home markets.

Why Have Markets Globalized So Rapidly?

Markets undergo the transformation from local to regional and then to global for several reasons. Rising consumer incomes; inexpensive air travel; instant communications via fax, television, telephone, and computer; and proliferating credit cards stimulate intercultural mixing and increased awareness of international products. As a result, market tastes often begin to homogenize, and brand awareness transfers rapidly across borders.

Many businesses seek growth and penetration in less developed markets, which often leads them outside the United States. For example, Armor All Products Corporation of Irvine, California, a $126 million company (sales) recently made a big push to sell its products for automobile maintenance internationally, because 57 percent of all automobiles are owned outside North America. A move to globalize has the benefit of moderating the effects of a U.S. business cycle downturn, since faster non-U.S. growth can carry the day. For example, GM and Ford each have 11 percent of the European car market, which cushions their earnings when the U.S. market goes into a tailspin, while Chrysler, with little share in Europe, has no such safety net on its earnings. A. T. Cross,[2] the upscale pen and pencil manufacturer, grew from $20 million in sales to over $200 million by putting its resources into markets outside the United States and sticking to this strategy throughout the 1980s. Colgate Palmolive has been more successful internationally than in the United States; almost two-thirds of Colgate's sales and profits are from operations abroad, and it holds a 42 percent market share in toothpaste outside the United States compared to Procter & Gamble's 20 percent. (In the United States, Procter & Gamble has a 34 percent share, compared to Colgate's 28 percent.)

The Pressure of Fixed Costs

Quite apart from seeking growth in greener pastures, companies seek productivity and profit returns from their investments and fixed costs.

Business is increasingly a fixed cost-return game, and the largest possible volumes must be sought to cover overhead. Product development costs are fixed costs expended in hopes of invention and its subsequent commercial exploitation. Manufacturing, with less labor content per unit output due to mechanization of formerly manual work, is also very much a fixed cost due to union contracts; machinery and automated factories require high volumes if they are to generate a payback on capital and fixed operating costs. Brand development via advertising is also a fixed cost activity; huge sums must be spent to develop and nurture a brand in anticipation of volume sales through which to cover these outlays. For instance Upjohn Company's Rogaine, a drug to assist bald men to grow hair back, has cost Upjohn $50 million per year to advertise despite total sales per year in 1989 of only $100 million. Clearly Upjohn must invest heavily up front in brand awareness before expecting to sell the volume of Rogaine required for a profit.

The setup costs of distribution and ongoing warehousing and the costs of customer branch service mandate that large market shares and global volumes be sought to pay back these investments.

Having multiple markets to sell into assists companies in balancing costs. For example, when the European market for one of Dow Chemical's solvents declined, the company shifted some of its idle German capacity to a product it had imported from Louisiana and Texas. By balancing supply–demand factory decisions worldwide, and using mathematical models, Dow boosted its average capacity utilization and kept its capital costs lower. (Dow's return on equity in 1988 was 14.2 percent, double that of BASF, Hoechst, Bayer, and DuPont. Its closest rival was Imperial Chemical Industries of Britain, with an 8.9 percent return on assets.[3])

A company that lacks global outlet for its production is at a severe scale disadvantage if its rivals are global players. For instance, a business such as Hewlett-Packard, which sells close to $12 billion a year, with 53 percent of sales outside the United States, must spend about $1.5 billion on research and development to stay ahead in its technologies. A smaller U.S. business spending a similar percentage of sales on research and development would be at a severe disadvantage if all its rivals were of Hewlett-Packard's global size and scale; it would simply have too small a market to be world-class in its research and development efforts. When Zenith Electronics skimped on necessary investments in new technology, Zenith Data, its computer subsidiary, lost $70 million and saw its global share of the laptop market plummet from 28 percent to 14 percent. Subaru (Fuji Heavy Industries), unable to attain stature as a global player in automobiles, was recently taken over by Nissan, which will try to revive the company's severely underutilized capacity and reverse its operating losses.

This phenomenon is one of the reasons the pharmaceutical

industry, a research-and-development-intensive business, today comprises either world-class giants or very small niche companies. Because a blockbuster drug can take $200 million and ten years to develop, there is no room for the mid-size businesses that lack the market scale to pay for the research and development necessary to bring new drugs to market. The niche companies survive by relying on their ability to cover markets too small to interest the giants, yet large enough to provide solid operating margins.

The Ability to Speed Product Development

Having global operations permits a company to accelerate product development by focusing and coordinating the talents of engineers, designers, and scientists in different locations to work simultaneously on different parts of a product's evolution. Each lab center does not need to diffuse and fog its focus. For instance, the Accord station wagon was designed at Honda's studio in California, based on technology from Honda's Tochigi, Japan, lab, and the car will be engineered and built at Marysville, Ohio.

Otis Elevator's newest Elevonic 411 high-tech elevator was developed in five nations—the doors in France, motor in Germany, small gears in Spain, motor drives in Japan, and computer system controls in the United States. Design costs were estimated to be $10 million lower than if Otis had tried to have only one of its centers develop the entire elevator.[4] In addition, Otis cut two years from its development cycle, from a four-year time frame to a two-year one. This allowed Otis to generate two additional years' sales volumes compared to its previous cycle times, a big advantage when products have relatively short life cycles prior to becoming obsolete.

The only way Airbus Industries could ever have become a player of global stature in the manufacture of aircraft was to utilize the talents of its four different consortium partners. Therefore, it organized itself so that its A300 and A310 wide-body jets are assembled in Toulouse, France, with wings from its British partner (British Aerospace), the fuselage from its German partner (Deutsche Airbus), the tailfin from its Spanish partner (Spanish Aerospace), and the cockpit from the French partner (French Aerospatiale).[5]

Clearly, good ideas and skills are not all headquartered in one nation. Having a global presence assists a company in finding the best talent and applying it rapidly in a coordinated way for the benefit of the whole.

The Corporation as a Brand

Of the top 200 advertised brands in the United States in 1989, 90 were corporate brands instead of individual product brands.[6] Figure 5-1 lists some of these corporate brands.

Well-known corporate trademarks assist companies in establishing reputations with global reach and take preeminence over specifically branded products or services. High corporate brand awareness translates into the ability to move across into new product categories while trading on the brand equity of the

Figure 5-1. A sampling of top advertised corporate brands in the United States (1988).

Service Companies	Product-Based Companies
McDonald's	IBM
American Express	Toyota
Sears	Hallmark
American Airlines	Goodyear
AT&T	General Electric
7-Eleven	Reebok
Midas	Upjohn
Toys "R" Us	Levi Strauss
Federal Express	GTE
MCI	Kodak
Disney	Canon
Kmart	Mercedes-Benz
Hertz	Nissan
Prudential	General Motors

Source: List compiled from data in "The Top 200 Brands," *Marketing and Media Decisions* (July 1990), pp. 36–38.

corporation as a whole. For example, Canon has moved from cameras to copiers, as has Minolta, while Sony has moved from Walkman radios (audio) to camcorders (video) while keeping the Sony name paramount. Honda has shifted from motorcycles to cars to chain saws on the strength of its corporate brand.

In one survey conducted in Europe, of the ten best-known brands, all were corporate brands, rather than specific models or products. They included Mercedes, Philips, Volkswagen, Rolls-Royce, Porsche, Coca-Cola, Ferrari, BMW, Michelin, and Volvo.

Procter & Gamble turned around its business in Japan in part by emphasizing its company name in its television advertising over the individual brands of its soap, detergents, and diapers. In the same vein, McDonald's familiar golden arches entice consumers to try its food in any global location, including new outlets in Russia and future planned sites in Eastern Europe.

Having a global corporate brand name with high recognition is of great benefit in getting distributors or dealers to take on the product line, since they feel more confident that the product will move off their shelves when consumer confidence in the company's reputation is very high. The corporate brand equity, in a sense, presells the product. The Japanese are particularly astute at emphasizing corporate branding. They span very diverse businesses, using monolithic branding. For instance, Mitsubishi is a brand identity that trademarks a bank, a car company, a manufacturer of aircraft, a manufacturer of consumer goods, and even a manufacturer of canned salmon. As one of the world's largest corporations, Mitsubishi believes in transferring its reputation for quality across all sorts of operations.

Global Focus of Competitors

Another reason globalization is occurring so rapidly is the ease of technology transfers among nations. U.S. semiconductor makers and machine-tool manufacturers have lost out to Japanese competitors because they failed to recognize how rapidly technology can transfer around the world. Rapid technology transfer often can transform an across-the-world faraway competitor into a very formidable class competitor, successfully selling into a company's home market. As technology transfer boundaries[7] fall as a result of increasingly open trade and improved communications, very few national markets can avoid the onslaught from aggressive external competitors.

This phenomenon, of course, is self-fulfilling. Organizations must pay attention to global rivals; in doing so, they must transform themselves into global competitors so they can strike back at a rival in its home market and remove any "safe-haven" profits it covets. This is especially true for U.S. businesses; if an international rival can wreak havoc in the U.S. market without worrying about retaliation on its own home ground, such market inroads by the rival will be all incremental profit (and these profits will be sizeable given the huge scale of the United States).

Being "competitor-focused" almost invariably motivates a business to think and act globally toward its key rivals. Groupe Bull of France recently set its sights on moving from number nine in world sales of computers to number five; in order to achieve its goal, it has had to spend considerably more time and money than previously in trying to beat rivals such as IBM, DEC, Hewlett-Packard, Olivetti, and Unisys. To get a bigger stake outside France, it bought Zenith Data Systems, a U.S.-based personal computer maker with $1.5 billion in sales. Similarly, when Electrolux of Sweden sought a larger global share of the appliance industry, it acquired Zanussi in Europe to become number one there and White Consolidated Industries in the United States to become number three in the U.S. market.

Trade Channel Power

Companies may seek to become global in size and scope, often through acquisition, because the customers to whom they sell have gotten bigger and smarter.

In Europe, for example, eight giant food retail chains, including Britain's Safeway Food Stores Ltd. and France's Casino, formed Associated Marketing Services, a buying group with international clout. The response to this move from the food manufacturers was to acquire larger shares in all European markets in categories important to them by buying up other companies. Philip Morris (U.S.), in order to compete with Unilever (Dutch) and Nestlé (Swiss) in Europe, bought out Jacob Suchard[8] and boosted its category clout in milk chocolate bars (Toblerone and Milka brands), coffee (Grand Mere and Jacques Vabre brands), and cocoa (Van Houten brand); as a result, Philip Morris's total dollar sales revenue in Europe doubled. Failure to take this step might have put Philip Morris in a weak negotiating position with buyers, who could have cut deals with alternative giants such as Nestlé and Unilever for prime shelf space and promotions. In the United States, one hundred chain stores now account for 80 percent of Procter & Gamble's grocery business, compared to 15 percent in 1970; these chains have no scruples about using their buying clout to the fullest possible extent.

Some trade channel middlemen have themselves become globally strong. Examples are Benetton, the $1.1 billion Italian apparel retailer; IKEA, the Swedish furniture retailer; and United Westburne, Inc., North America's largest integrated electrical wholesaler ($2.6 billion in 1989), which controls the third and fourth largest electrical wholesalers in France—CGE Distribution ($600 million in size) and Groupelec ($300 million in size). Westburne intends to formulate "cooperative global strategies," according to the news release that announced the takeover of these French businesses.[9]

Information power has given trade channels extra clout in dealing with suppliers. J. Sainsbury, a world-leading supermarket in own-label marketing, knows from its scanners how its products move on-promotion, in only four hours. The manufacturing suppliers who sell to it don't have this same shelf-movement information for six weeks since they buy it from third parties.[10] Some retailers are expanding their already strong global presence as a result of the opening up of Eastern Europe markets. For example, Woolworth, the chain store operator, has 284 variety stores and 154 specialty stores such as Footlocker in Western Europe. It plans to add eight to ten stores in eastern Germany in 1991 and hopes to expand to Poland, where it had thirty stores prior to World War I.

Issues in Globalized Marketing

Having a global mindset and marketing organization does not mean that cultural differences in markets can be ignored and that total standardization of market mix elements can be implemented regardless of nation. There are, after all, telling differences between markets that cannot be ignored or minimized. Gillette's TRAC II razors didn't sell well in the Middle East, where fewer potential male customers shave. There are formidable challenges in globalizing marketing, given differences among nations in language, literacy, religion, customs, history, and governmental controls. Yet, despite these challenges, standardization in marketing is often feasible across quite varied regions. IBM, for instance, used to alter its advertising campaigns for personal computers for every different nation in Europe. Today, IBM's advertising is uniform in image and text across Europe. Its 1991 television ads for its PS/1 cost $2 million less in creative and production costs than would have been the case had it continued to customize its ads for each European country.

Global marketing involves three imperatives:

1. The commercial exploitation of good marketing ideas on a global scale wherever possible, regardless of origin.

2. The astute standardization of high fixed-cost elements of marketing across world markets wherever this standardization does not reduce potential global profits or market share that more customized marketing programs might provide. As long as the cost savings from standardized programs outweigh lost profits from marketing customization, the decision to globalize market mix elements is sound.

3. Global marketing requires implementation with a "top-down–bottom-up" team approach that values and blends the local management experience and knowledge of those closest to customers (country managers) with specifically valuable headquarters resources and expertise (product division or functional managers). Unless the field managers and headquarters marketing personnel have fruitful ongoing input into the soundness of marketing strategies and executional tactics, the globalization of marketing will not work very well.

If headquarters product managers feel and act as if they have a monopoly on good plans and programs, strong capable field managers will leave the company to seek out positions where their feedback, ideas, and local market expertise will be valued. On the other hand, if the field personnel dominate strategy and program design discussions, no coherent coordinated strategies to defeat global competitors operating in multiple markets are likely to emerge, and few efforts will be made to optimize total marketing spending across markets and to spot those good ideas that are shared between regions.

Field and headquarters marketing personnel must be equal partners for globalization to succeed. If they pull in opposite directions, the company cannot pursue opportunities quickly because of the infighting; if one organization dominates the other, either critical national marketing differences will be ignored (to the company's possible peril) or so much local tailoring of programs will occur that simultaneous product launches will become impossible, leaving some markets wide open to preemption by faster-moving, more "together" competitors.

Exploiting Ideas With Global Scale

The economic argument for exploiting good product or service ideas globally is obvious. Sticking to one's own national market and even dominating it provides only a very small overall percentage of world market potential. For instance, a 40 percent share of the U.S. market (and 40 percent often represents the market share ceiling enjoyed by any business in a variety of industries) still represents only 15 percent of world demand.

France would not contain the world's largest manufacturer of ballpoint pens or the world's second largest automotive tire manufacturer if BIC and Michelin had exploited the ideas of disposable pens and radial tires respectively only in their home market of France. Similarly, Boeing and Caterpillar, Inc., went overseas early out of economic necessity.

Nestlé created instant coffee more than fifty years ago and exploited this product idea with such patience and marketing skill that it still dominates as the top seller in most nations of the world. Sales of Nescafé are still growing rapidly in Britain and Japan, nations where tea drinking has been a tradition for centuries. Nescafé has half the market in Britain and is growing rapidly in Japan, where coffee is considered a luxury gift item, often substituted for chocolates or flowers as a birthday or dinner party gift.[11] Nestlé has also made a great success of its Lean Cuisine brand of low-calorie frozen dinners on both sides of the Atlantic.

Failure to exploit good ideas with wide global geographic appeal is as serious a form of marketing myopia as defining one's core business wrongly and finding one's business wiped out by competitors one did not recognize or acknowledge. For instance, in 1979 Henkel believed its Sista product line of do-it-yourself sealants had market potential well beyond the company's home market of Germany. It put together a standard marketing program and sought the endorsement of its European marketing teams for the program's implementation by subsidizing the ad and promotion spending on the new line for the first year from headquarters, rather than from the individual country budgets. Country managers, initially leery of going along with the Sista standard program because of its costs and their individually small national markets, went along enthusiastically once this risk-cost sharing proposal was offered. By 1982, Sista was successful not only in Europe but in fifty-two countries worldwide. Failure to exploit the Sista line globally would have been not only a waste of a good idea but of sunk marketing program cost elements that had already been expended to make the product a success in Germany.

What to Standardize and What to Tailor

Marketing consists of fourteen key decision-making elements that can be standardized globally, customized locally, or fall somewhere between the two extremes. These fourteen elements include:

1. The preparation and acceptance of the marketing plan by management.
2. The design of the product or service and its key features.
3. The brand naming of the product or service.
4. The product positioning selected for the product; that is, the basis upon which the company will attempt to differ-

entiate its offering from its rivals to its selected target market.
5. The packaging of the product, including the packaging graphics, shape, color, size, and construction.
6. The advertising theme line and copy chosen for the product or service.
7. The preferred ad media chosen to influence target customers favorably.
8. The pricing levels and trade discounts selected to market the product to both end customers and trade retailers, wholesalers, or distributors.
9. The distribution channel network preferred by the company for its product's sale.
10. The sales promotion choices the company wishes to make to boost product volume sales throughout the year.
11. The customer service standards and sales policies the company will adopt toward its customers, including standards in order handling and fulfillment, terms of payment, and policies governing credit and returned goods.
12. The warranty policies the company will promote and stand behind.
13. The sales aids the company to display or demonstrate the product in its best light, and to assist and motivate both its sales force and its customers.
14. The marketing support service policies it will pursue in such matters as the selection and appointment of ad agencies, market research houses, sales promotion agencies, and other specialized agencies (trade show designers, direct marketing houses, package design consultants, premium and incentive consultants).

The operating pressure to standardize any one of these elements is a function of the degree to which the costs of the element are largely fixed and to which economies of scale are possible through standardization. If the element represents a large percentage of the cost of the total marketing effort, pressures to standardize will be greatest. Operating effectiveness issues such as consistent image control or protection of trademarks often create pressure for standardization, as well.

Generally speaking, pressures to standardize globally are highest in the areas of:

- Product design
- Product positioning (the very core of marketing strategy)
- Product branding
- Advertising theming
- Packaging

Each of these elements (with the exception of packaging) represents high fixed development costs. Packaging design, while it is a variable cost, is frequently standardized to function as the company's "silent salesman," offering a consistent image across national borders (which share cross-border distribution channels and ad media coverage). Using multilingual packaging can enable a company to serve huge market areas with only one design.

Of course, standardizing product design often excludes some potential customers. When Canon designed a photocopier for global sale, its design precluded its use with some sizes of Japanese paper. Food or household products must often be slightly modified to conform to specific tastes or habits. Procter & Gamble experienced this situation firsthand in Japan, having to customize many of its detergents. Coca-Cola has had to customize Diet Coke for the Japanese by adding more fructose.

Pressure to customize by nation is most prevalent in:

- Pricing and trade discounts
- Sales promotion spending choices
- Ad media choices
- Distribution network choices
- Customer service standards
- Sales policies (e.g., payment terms)
- Sales aids

Sales promotion and sales aids vary by nation because there are often few short-term sales incentive programs (contests, trade deals) with either universal appeal or significant scale advantages.

(For instance, couponing must often be customized by language.) Globalizing pricing, sales terms, and trade discounts doesn't make sense unless pricing consistency is necessary due to global contracts with worldwide customers. By pricing on a customized market-by-market basis, a company gains two advantages: It can cross-subsidize its pricing, using profits from high-share markets to penetrate low-share markets by lowering price, and it can test the upper limit of customer price sensitivity and assure itself that it captures maximum profits per segment by pricing to individual markets.

Distribution and media choices are idiosyncratic by market because so few identical networks exist across regions. For instance, media prevalence and regulations vary greatly among European countries. There are 46 different newspapers per million Swiss in Switzerland, yet in Austria a single page ad in *Kronenzeitung* reaches half of all Austrians.[12] Billboards in France are double the per capita density of England; in Spain, billboards are very restricted on inter-urban highways. Denmark introduced its first-ever commercial TV channel as recently as October 1988.

Distribution network similarities across regions are, more often than not, limited by the penetration of various products in these markets, which reflect individual national consumer spending priorities. For instance, consider the market penetration of videocassette recorders and microwave ovens in parts of Europe. In the United Kingdom, more than 50 percent of households own VCRs, while in Greece only 5 percent do. Microwave ovens have penetrated 30 percent of all households in Britain but only 2 percent of Spanish households.[13] So any company attempting to duplicate distribution channel choices for these two products in different countries will find the number, skill, and types of retail dealers for them as different as night and day.

Globalized distribution channel choices are always hampered by agent, wholesaler, distributor, and retailer network variations. Lego, the Danish construction toy manufacturer, uses a variety of distribution methods to go to market, even though it markets its globally identical products with similar target positionings.

Customer service standards for functions such as delivery, order placement, and turnaround are also difficult to standardize globally because customer expectations for these elements vary so much depending on the extent of urbanization and transportation infrastructure development in each country. In Belgium, a small country, 89 percent of the population lives in cities of 150,000 or more persons, whereas only 33 percent of Portugal's population and 71 percent of Italy's are so situated. Customers' expectations concerning product availability, ease of ordering, and promptness of delivery are all conditioned by the physical ease of access to them, based on existing road networks, distances from cities, and proximity to organized chain stores and urban shopping outlets with efficient stocking practices.

Global Advertising

Global brands have been helped along not merely by cost-scale advantages; advertising agencies have consolidated to provide their marketing services for global clients. Recognizing that landing a global account represents "megabucks," agencies have scrambled to help advertisers consolidate their purchase of creative and to coordinate their media buying.

To accommodate the needs of global manufacturers for globally developed ads, the agencies have pursued the logical course of themselves becoming global in scope. By organizing to meet the needs of global clients, agencies have probably hastened the pace of globalization.

For example, three huge agencies now dominate the global landscape. They are Saatchi and Saatchi (U.K.), which combined several agencies to become the world's largest; WPP Group (U. K.), which operates in fifty nations and includes on its global account list Nestlé, Citicorp, Pepsico, Kodak, and Kraft-General Foods; and Ommicom Group, formed from the merger of BBDO, Doyle Dane Bernbach, and Needham Harper Worldwide. Whether these mega-agencies can provide clients with the services and creativity demanded of them in their current enlarged size remains to be seen. Creativity and responsiveness often suffer as agencies grow larger and more bureaucratic; in addition, some creative talent turnover can occur if people sense a loss of autonomy in their creative activities. The financing of much of this agency merger activity has also left these companies deeply in debt and strapped financially. In addition, it may be possible to preserve globalized ad programs without using only one agency, simply by using a series of agencies allied in one location.

While it is often desirable to brand products such as Swatch or Benetton globally by name, it isn't always feasible. Procter & Gamble sells its successful Always brand sanitary napkins under that name in the United States and Europe but uses the brand name Whisper in Japan, where *always* doesn't translate well. Whisper is the leader in feminine protection products in the Japanese market.[14] When Playtex tried to brand its new bra WOW globally, it found the name had to be translated into Traumbugel in Germany (meaning "dream wire") and Alas in Spain. Exact brand name and connotations simply aren't always possible in other languages, and literal translations sometimes have less punch in the context of other words in a different language. Needless to say, WOW wasn't a whopping universal success as a global brand. Polaroid sells its cameras and accessories in the United States under the brand Spectra System while using the brand name Image System in Europe for the identical products.

Global Product Warranties

Product warranties often represent a unique and creative marketing tool by which a company can gain market share and reputation. Warranties are a creative tool because a company can alter any number of elements, including the breadth of repairs or components covered, the length of time the warranty covers, and the conditions under which the warranty can be invoked, to appeal to a buyer. A company can differentiate itself from its rivals by offering unique warranty provisions—an all-inclusive warranty, a lifetime warranty, a "no-questions asked" replacement warranty, a no-deductible warranty. When Chrysler boosted its power train warranty from two years or 24,000 miles to seven years or 70,000 miles in the early 1980s, it greatly boosted the appeal of its autos and vans.

Standardizing all warranty elements globally communicates unlimited faith in a company's products. However, if competitive conditions or market needs differ, this policy may not make sense; such standardizing may offer far more than is necessary competitively in some markets and too little in other markets.

On luxury goods sold globally, such as Rolex watches, a global warranty often makes sense. On products with varying ownership cycles or differences in operating conditions, a more tailored market-by-market warranty offer is more appropriate. Polaroid offers longer camera warranties in Europe than in the United States because Europeans tend to own their cameras longer. Varying warranties by market has the additional advantage of protecting dealer networks by market, since the warranty is more easily declared inoperable if a global standard warranty is not in place and the product is purchased from an unauthorized dealer.

The Trend Toward Global Sales Promotion

Sales promotion has almost always been a local affair; national marketing managers differed in their choice of promotion tools to boost volume sales both by promotion type (sampling, couponing, contests, price packs, rebates,) and by timing. Their choices resulted in part from differences in trade channel or end-user preferences for certain promotions, the market's state of development, and the types of regulations placed upon sales promotion activities in different countries. To illustrate, coupons are not a widely accepted promotion vehicle in Japan, where Japanese consumers are often embarrassed to redeem them in stores. In a nation such as Malaysia, contests are allowed only if they involve skill, not chance—so "Instant Win"-type contests cannot be used as they are in North America.[15]

As sales promotion spending escalates to exceed brand advertising, companies are increasingly attempting to find promotional vehicles with global appeal and scope. These global promotion vehicles often take the form of sporting events, such as World Cup skiing, tennis, or soccer or the Olympic Games. Other promotional vehicles that span multiple countries are charity or cause-related events such as the "Human Rights Now!" music concerts, which were cosponsored by Reebok and Amnesty International and staged in fourteen different nations. Some businesses select other cause-related promotion ventures with global range, such as the International Wildlife Fund. In such a case, the business donates some specified share of the purchase price of its products to the fund, while advertising the connection heavily. Its brands then become associated with global organizations working for an appealing transnational cause.

In many instances, companies moving to globalize promotion spending do so in a way that allows local country managers flexibility in program execution. For instance, a global sponsor of the Olympic Games might allow its worldwide subsidiaries wide latitude in terms of exploiting the Olympic connection for local trade, consumer, or sales force promotions. The only common element between promotional content in, say, Mexico and Brazil may be the umbrella sponsorship and the access it provides to Olympic symbol usage, such as the official Olympic rings and specific city site insignia. All of these efforts to provide brand umbrella frameworks for sales promotion represent attempts to concentrate marketing spending force in an area typically beset by fragmented focus and splintered piecemeal spending programs.

Time Compression and Globalization of Products

Another issue that promotes globalization in product development is the advent of time-compressed competition. Managements no longer have the luxury of long head starts before competition matches their product lead. In this fast-paced race to stay ahead of the competition, managements cannot afford to adapt every new product specifically for each country. It simply takes too long (and costs too much in engineering, research, development, and market testing).

In order to meet the stern challenge of speeding product development, companies are often forced into some nontraditional kinds of activities. For instance, Ford Motor Company hooked up with Mazda to design and engineer its new Escort, to be marketed globally by both companies under different names. The car, built in twelve different assembly plants, was produced at a saving of $1 billion in engineering costs to Ford, because Ford had Mazda engineer the inside of the vehicle at the same time as Ford engineered the outside. The cost saving may turn out to be less important than the fact that Ford hit all of its tight time deadlines in its drive to have a world car designed and ready for market release in 1990, despite major setbacks along the way (an escalating yen and tougher mileage requirements laid on by Washington regulators midway through the car's development).[16]

In the trend toward seeking more global customers, are service businesses often forced to operate on a twenty-four hour day. For example, the venerable New York Stock Exchange is in the process of planning around-the-clock operation so that stocks may be traded from any time zone in the world. This move is in response to global competition for stock trades from companies such as Reuters, which supplies 200,000 broker-trading terminals around the world with financial information. These terminals are now equipped technically to allow traders to execute buy-sell orders instantaneously on the same network. Failure of the NYSE to operate on a twenty-four hour basis would keep it from participating in more than 15 million daily share trades placed on U.S. stocks from overseas buyers, using methods such as the Reuters network.[17]

Motivating Organizational Teamwork

It is axiomatic that as more parts of the marketing mix are standardized for global implementation, subsidiary managements will feel a loss of autonomy in the practice of their marketing. Yet the role and value of country marketing managements in a globalized business is critical. They often spot local market opportunities that can translate well and be adapted around the world. Unilever's South African operation, for instance, came up with the brand Impulse, a body spray that is now sold globally. Subs monitor local competition; only by studying their input can headquarters business planners become aware of competitor strategies in different areas and the emerging total picture. Local managers are closest to customer needs, and, by feeding customer comments back to headquarters, they provide suggestions that can be followed up to enhance products, customer services, merchandising plans, and advertising campaigns. At 3M, local subs are encouraged to create new businesses that are then advertised globally within 3M so that other subs can adopt them. 3M's Flip-Frame transparency holders became a global success this way after its Swedish sub came up with the new product idea. Despite globalization, there still exists the need to continuously improve products, ad copy, positioning themes, logistical response times, and other components of the marketing mix. In fact, as companies push their organizations for more quality in all operations, improving marketing elements to stand the test of the toughest market regardless of global location can push the company to higher and higher performance standards. Why benchmark the U.S. quality standards if other customers elsewhere are more demanding?

Businesses combining the most effective systems of global market planning with subsidiary execution embrace several operating principles:

1. They encourage maximum exchange of ideas between the subs and headquarters with joint meetings, newsletters, and mutual visits. Such communication ensures that everyone gets listened to, and cross-national cooperative successes can be publicized and expanded.

2. Their headquarters don't attempt to control all the spending. When British Airways moved to its award-winning globalized ad campaign, it still left enough ad budget money within country managers' control for them to promote special fares, destinations, and other inducements. In fact, the ratio of total sub compared to total headquarters ad spending was 1½ to 1 (£18 million sterling versus £13 million).

3. They encourage the liberal career movement of marketing managers between headquarters and field subsidiary (or regional) assignments. In this way, managers learn to understand and appreciate each marketing perspective on a firsthand "gut" level. It's tough to second-guess other managers, in the head office or in the field, when one has personally experienced their particular situation.

4. They often provide dual performance measurements, so that country managers and headquarters division marketing personnel must maximize not just product growth/penetration or country sales growth/profitability respectively, but must keep their eye on both measures if they hope to get ahead in their careers. Matrix P&L management is necessary.

5. Astute globalized companies tend to formalize task forces or teams to hammer out specific pan-regional programs, and these teams are equally balanced with specialist functional staff members from headquarters and the line marketing subsidiary countries. Such teams can then maximize top-down–bottom-up idea sharing and disband when they have completed their limited mandate. This limited duration mandate prevents the problem of the team's beginning to assume line operating profit and loss responsibilities that run the risk of undermining chain-of-command accountability.

Procter & Gamble has successfully used Euro-Brand teams composed of multiple country managers as well as specialists with more of a pan-European perspective, such as technical managers or division heads for entire regions of Europe.

Industrial Compared With Consumer Companies

While many of the products that are marketed globally are consumer products, such as Swatch, Coca-Cola, Levi's, Rolex, and so forth, industrial companies actually stand as good a chance to globalize their offerings as do makers of watches, blue jeans, or soft drinks.

The reasons for this are varied, but they include the fact that industrial products (those bought by other businesses) are often less culture-bound than foods, clothing, and other household products. A great many products used by businesses are standardized in key operating features; this is the case for computers, factory robots, and other sophisticated high-tech office and plant equipment. Such standardized features make worldwide selling highly feasible. Honeywell's controls work as well in Nigeria and Brazil as in France.

Purchasing agents acting on behalf of businesses base their buying decisions on more systematic and rational criteria than do many consumers buying for ego or image identification reasons. There is a great deal of commonality among purchasing agents toward industrial products that cuts across national boundaries; a purchasing agent buying machine tools for a factory in Australia probably uses criteria similar to those used by a purchasing agent for a similarly configured factory in Sweden, Singapore, or Ireland. So as long as a manufacturer of machine tools can meet the high quality specifications demanded by the purchasing agent's factory, it will be usually given a chance to bid for the order, regardless of where its home base of operations is located. This explains why a company like Apple Computer, with its unique Macintosh desktop publishing technology, could attract global sales so quickly; business purchasers are always on the lookout for unique products and have the sophistication to seek them out and arrange for their purchase, delivery, and installation.

In addition, while many consumer products depend on mass advertising to enable them to reach a level of brand awareness that makes global sales feasible, industrial companies can use much more selective means to reach their key customers (which often represent the bulk of usage for their products). These select media include sales reps or agents, distributors, direct mail, trade shows, international trade fairs, and print ads in specific trade journals. Each of these media or personal sales methods makes the global acceptance of industrial products much less of a high-ante poker game than that for consumer mass-advertised items.

An excellent example of an industrial company that has gained significant market standing globally by emphasizing a highly selective program of key account marketing and application specific product design is Johnson Electric Industries Manufacturing Ltd.[18] Johnson does more than $100 million a year in sales in micromotors and is the world's second largest independent producer of small motors for cameras, hairdryers, cordless tools, electric car aerials, and small kitchen appliances. Founded in 1959 in Hong Kong, Johnson began by making inexpensive standardized micromotors for toys. By working with global companies such as Black & Decker (its largest account), Kodak, and Sunbeam, Johnson has moved its product mix into more customized, higher-value-added motors for products such as Kodak's disk camera and Krups' citrus juicers. Concentrating on selected target industries such as small-appliance makers, Johnson has convinced many manufacturers to stop manufacturing these motors themselves in favor of sourcing high-quality motors at reasonable prices from Johnson. Johnson has found the appeal of customized high-quality component motors for such customers to be universal, especially among original equipment manufacturers who pride themselves on their quality reputations.

As Johnson illustrates, global industrial marketing need not always require large dollar spending on trade shows, print ads, or sales forces, as long as a company can establish a quality product and service reputation that cuts across borders. If it can then concentrate its marketing resources on those parts of a global market that are quality sensitive rather than price shoppers, it can often succeed in gaining a large global market share. (Johnson had net pretax profits of 20 percent on its 1988 sales and its dollar sales growth since 1982 has quadrupled.)

The Niche Company

Diversified global companies such as Procter & Gamble, DuPont, Nestlé, 3M, Royal Dutch Shell, Mitsubishi, General Electric, Siemens, Sony, Philips, and Black & Decker have clearly established a presence in a great many worldwide markets. Most have not only diversified products, customer sets, and research and development centers but globally integrated manufacturing and managements rich in international operating experience.

Does this mean that the small niche specialist company has a more difficult chore in globalizing its presence because it has fewer resources and fewer products over which to spread its fixed marketing costs? Not necessarily. It is more difficult if the niche company is in an industry where scale economics in research and development, engineering, and manufacturing are critical to success, such as the manufacture of cars, petrochemicals, tires, large household appliances, and farm machinery. In these industries, consolidations have cut the number of small share players significantly; a company such as Fiat, overly dependent on its home market for the bulk of its car sales, may need to merge or face a bleak future in the global game of car manufacturing.

In businesses, however, where capital intensity is somewhat lower and value is added less in the upstream operations such as the lab or factory, a smaller niche company can often expand globally quite successfully. Examples include specialized retailers such as Britain's The Body Shop, Loctite (the world's preeminent global marketer of anaerobic adhesives for industry), and Hyster, a specialized manufacturer of narrow-aisle high-reach forklifts. These organizations have concentrated their resources in unique downstream marketing activities, from specializing their sales reps ("Loctite"), to unique product design, ("Hyster"), to a one-of-a-kind retailing formula for cosmetics ("The Body Shop").

As mass markets break up, with jaded buyers demanding more variety in products, it should be increasingly possible for the small niche company to duplicate its home product successes globally. For instance, Cenogenics, a small U.S.-based marketer of diagnostic products for hospital testing (pregnancy tests, tests for arthritis, mono, colon cancer, strep infections), has already managed to globalize its product sales to more than $3 million in ten years by selecting and targeting selected countries with its unique high-quality offerings and professional staff.[19]

Guidelines for Global Success

Global marketing is the process of leveraging a company's international size and geographic scope to outperform its competition. And when it works, it can work beautifully. For instance, Johnson Wax improved its European market share by rationalizing the number of personal care and cleaning products it sold in Europe and then standardizing the branding and product formulations for these products. It reduced its product varieties, which allowed it to have fewer but longer production runs per product and to obtain larger raw material discounts. It cut finished-goods inventories and factory personnel while boosting its brand presence in Europe. Savings in plant personnel were approximately 50 percent, while inventory savings were roughly 20 percent. So doing business globally can really boost cost efficiency and branding effectiveness.

But global marketing can also bomb out. Parker Pen centralized its marketing in the hands of global marketers in its head office in the mid-1980s, centralized its manufacturing, and standardized its packaging, pricing, promotions, and advertising. Its 154 local country managers around the world, who had previously controlled these decisions, were expected to follow tight edicts from the head office and were required to deal with only one ad agency. Needless to say, these managers rebelled; when lackluster operating results followed, Parker Pen's senior management was forced to resign.

Analysis of global marketing programs has synthesized those conditions that increase the probability of success.[20] Successful global marketers (in contrast to unsuccessful ones) made certain that they got five things right when designing or executing programs:

1. *They appointed a champion for the program who could overcome initial country manager resistance.* This champion succeeded because of excellent interpersonal and persuasion skills; widely respected multinational work experience and a proven track record in marketing in subsidiaries; and analytic abilities in defining the marketing opportunity and determining which parts of the marketing mix should be standardized globally and where local autonomy should be preserved.

Digital Equipment was able to rationalize and standardize key sales management tasks in seventeen European operations, despite initial local opposition, because it chose a champion for the project who had just these stellar qualifications and skills.

2. *They tested globalized programs on a smaller geographic scale prior to global roll-out.* In every successful case, the global soundness of the program was demonstrated and local country opposition overcome by a test in more than just one market. The test educated different subs about the program's merits. Because the test was conducted beyond the home country's borders, it had added credibility.

Henkel's successful globalization of its do-it-yourself adhesives branding under the umbrella brand Pattex owed a large part of its acceptance to the initial test of the program in Henkel's three major markets—Germany, Austria, and Belgium.

3. *They involved local subsidiaries in providing suggestions about program content and saw that the feedback was listened to by the designers of the program.* Although such consultations were often time-consuming and acrimonious, they helped ensure that global programs would not fail for reasons of less-than-optimum program design or lack of commitment from the subs.

4. *They designed a plan for team coordination of implementation.*
The team, which consisted of representatives of the largest subs,
was senior enough to know how to get the programs implemented; was given resources to pull off the launch; and was given
top-management recognition as a separate team with status inside the larger international organization structure.

5. *They provided the subs with flexibility in many of the executional
details.* Marketing operations dealing with customers need to be
decentralized so that decisions can be made faster and better
without having to go through a headquarters bureaucracy. Programs in which subs had no autonomy at all on a long list of
marketing tasks often failed. Strict control over program elements
was maintained only on a short list of strategic tasks, not on
complete laundry lists of each and every marketing practice
detail. Johnson Wax described such a global implementation
process with the slogan, "As unified as possible, as diversified as
necessary."

Globalized Marketing—Big Opportunities, Big Risks

When businesses truly market globally, their sales prospects are
altered completely. Consider the cases of Oregon-based Nike
Shoe and Massachusetts-based Reebok International. Once content with dominating the U.S. market for athletic shoes, they are
now going global with concerted attacks for market share in
Europe, where they are competing against Adidas and Puma, the
big names in sports shoes on that continent. They are signing up
sports celebrities in Europe to promote their shoes, expanding
distribution, and advertising very aggressively to get a bigger
chunk of the $5 billion European market. For instance, Nike will
spend $39 million to advertise in Europe, an increase of 44 percent
over 1990. Adidas and Puma are vulnerable because of both
unfocussed marketing and poor service to the shoe trade. Adidas
has marketed too many shoe models (1,200 designs) and has had
chronic delivery problems, while Puma has suffered from ongoing cash flow problems and a new management start-up. Both
were vulnerable, and Nike and Reebok succeeded in stealing

share. Nike's European sales hit over $500 million in 1990 and
Reebok's rose to $380 million, both up 100 percent over 1989
levels. If per capita spending on sports shoes in Europe approxi-
mates U.S. levels (ten dollars in the United States as compared
with three dollars in Europe), Nike and Reebok could potentially
double their U.S. company sales in the years ahead simply by
penetrating the huge, and somewhat untapped, European market. These companies are betting that use of athletic shoes will
spread in Europe and catch on as streetwear instead of being seen
as only for athletic use. As evidence of Nike's belief in a globalized approach, it has launched its Air 180 shoe with a $20 million
television campaign in fifteen cities around the world—its first
truly global product launch.

On the downside, when a company has successfully branded
and marketed its products globally and then a miscue occurs, the
mistake takes on global proportions instead of being a localized
problem. Consider the case of Perrier,[21] the French mineral water
company. On sale in more than 110 nations, the Perrier brand is
a huge global success enjoying more than a 40 percent market
share in the largest markets of the United States, United Kingdom, and Europe. The company has developed the market for
sparkling water to the point where Perrier is synonymous with
the product category, much like Kleenex (a Kimberly-Clark
brand) is for facial tissue. Perrier has built up a large range of
bottle sizes, cans, and offshoot products such as its "twist"-
flavored mineral waters.

All of a sudden, on February 10, 1990, in isolated purity tests
conducted in North Carolina, minute traces (six parts per billion)
of benzene were revealed. The Perrier U.S. subsidiary, fearing a
backlash from health-minded consumers because of benzene's
carcinogenic links, decided to recall the product from retail
shelves.

News of the product recall spread like wildfire through the
worldwide press, and both Perrier U.K. and Perrier's headquarters in France were forced to undertake similar product testing
immediately. When traces of benzene showed up, Perrier had to
confront the problem of a worldwide product recall. On February
15, five days after the North Carolina test results surfaced, Perrier
took out full-page newspaper ads across the world to announce

the total recall of its water, which in the United Kingdom's case alone represented the withdrawal and return of 40 million bottles.

Through swift action in tracking down the benzene contamination source (a filter used to purify carbon dioxide in its factory) and open communication with the press, the public, and trade accounts, Perrier was able to regain much of its lost market share within seven to eight months.

This case illustrates how the high visibility that accompanies globally successful marketers carries with it high vulnerability should a disaster such as Perrier's occur. The only response possible in such situations is to have ready a crisis management strategy to ensure that individual subsidiaries act in concert to preserve the integrity of the company's brand equity around the world. In a global marketplace, where instant communication occurs in the world press, no sensible options exist for the astute marketer other than to handle such a crisis with candor; forthright, definitive action; and trust that the loyal brand buyers can be won back over time.

Notes

1. W. J. Holstein, S. Reed, J. Kapstein, T. Vogel, and J. Weber, "The Stateless Corporation," *Business Week* (May 14, 1990), pp. 98–105. For more details on the sales and profits of global companies, see "The Global 1000," *Business Week* (July 16, 1990), pp. 111–136.
2. Ira Magaziner, "How to Win the New Global Wars," *Boardroom Reports* (October 15, 1989), pp. 9–10.
3. "Dow Draws Its Matrix Again—and Again, and Again," *The Economist* (August 5, 1989), p. 55. In 1988, Dow led in all categories of productivity, from net profit on sales to return on equity, return on assets, and sales per employee.
4. W. J. Holstein et al., op. cit., p. 101.
5. H. Perlmutter and D. Heenan, "Cooperate to Compete Globally," *Harvard Business Review* (March–April 1986), p. 147.
6. "The Top 200 Brands," *Marketing and Media Decisions* (July 1990), pp. 36–38.

7. T. Leuliette, "Can Technology Go Global?" *Industry Week* (July 16, 1990), p. 63.

8. J. Templeman and A. Melcher, "Supermarket Darwinism: The Survival of the Fattest," *Business Week* (July 9, 1990), p. 42.

9. "Westburne, Allies Work on Worldwide Thrust," *Toronto Star* (June 22, 1990), p. F7.

10. "Management Brief: Still Trying," *The Economist* (October 7, 1989), p. 93.

11. M. Alpert and A. D. Smith, "Nestlé Shows How to Gobble Markets," *Fortune* (January 16, 1989), p. 76.

12. *Viewpoint* (an Ogilvy & Mather publication) (March–April 1990), pp. 28, 29.

13. Ibid., p. 27.

14. B. Dumaine, "Procter & Gamble Rewrite the Marketing Rules," *Fortune* (November 6, 1989), p. 48.

15. K. Kashani and J. Quelch, "Can Sales Promotion Go Global?" *Business Horizons* (May–June, 1990), p. 39.

16. J. Treece and A. Borrus, "How Ford and Mazda Shared the Driver's Seat," *Business Week* (March 26, 1990), pp. 94, 96.

17. G. Weiss, "Stock Around the Clock," *Business Week* (July 2, 1990), pp. 30, 31.

18. A. Tanzer, "Small Motors, Big Profits," *Forbes* (July 11, 1989), pp. 85, 86.

19. J. Cohen, "Small Firm Earns Big Growth Through Exporting Savvy," *Management Review* (August 1990), pp. 25–28.

20. Kamran Kashani, "Why Does Global Marketing Work—or Not Work?" *European Management Journal* vol. 8, no. 2 (June 1990), pp. 150–155.

21. "Perrier's Painful Period," *Management Today* (U.K.) (August 1990), pp. 72–73.

6

Quality in Marketing: Putting the Customer First, Last, and Everywhere in Between

Better to lose money than trust.

Robert Bosch
(Believed in quality first and
founded Germany's ninth
largest industrial company—
world leaders in brakes, auto
lights, and car components.)

Demonstrating superior product and service quality boosts every key performance dimension in a company. Superior quality improves profits and return on investment because the company is less vulnerable to price wars, can command higher prices while keeping its market share, and can count on customers' loyalty, which boosts factory utilization and lowers marketing expenses per dollar of volume. Quality leadership also boosts growth, since customers are attracted by the better value they can get compared to the products offered by rivals.

Interestingly a preoccupation with cost cutting can also boost profits and return on investment. But if such cost cuts erode quality in the eyes of customers, eventually this strategy boomerangs. Schlitz in the early 1970s reduced its brewing costs on beer by switching to cheaper ingredients and a shorter brewing cycle, which cut its labor costs per barrel. By 1973 its sales and return on equity exceeded Anheuser-Busch's. However, by 1976, customers had discovered the erosion in quality, and Schlitz's market share began to fall, dropping from number one in the United States to number seven; its stock price went from $69 in 1974 to $5 in 1981. Even though it tried to recover its quality image in 1978 by reformulating its beer, it simply couldn't regain its former status as a quality beer in customers' eyes.

Given the compelling evidence that a superior quality image boosts financial returns, why do many companies fail to go all-out in pursuit of quality? The reason is that quality, to many companies, is synonymous with conformance to tight product tolerances, often expressed in defects per thousand units, rather than with a more customer-centered view of quality in which customer-based quality expectations are regularly monitored and exceeded by all parts of the organization (not just the factory). For instance, offering computers with impressive technical product superiority counts only if customers view this as *the* critical buying criterion. IBM's personal computers did well despite the technical superiority of other competitors' personal computers, simply because customers' idea of quality encompassed a broader view than just conformance to tight operating specifications. Customers like to buy from computer suppliers who will be around in ten years. They want processing power but also supplier staying power.

Customer-centered quality must always consider all the influences customers see as comprising a total quality offering, including many measures beyond product performance per se. Since the quality rating that counts is the customers' internal measure of perfection, it is possible to have several levels of quality in a market, depending upon the type or segment of customers and what attributes these segments value most highly.

For instance, Whirlpool markets three levels of quality appliances: high level to the upper end of the market with their Kitchenaid brand, middle-level quality under the Whirlpool label, and a more modest quality line under the Roper brand name.

Because customers' needs change over time and their expectations are altered by competitors' offerings, it is vital to measure customer quality assessments constantly. A one-time measurement or a nonsegmented approach to needs can mislead a company quite badly. For example, even though General Motors is improving its cars' quality, its Japanese rivals are doing so even more rapidly in the eyes of many customers and are doing so in some segments quite dramatically (for instance, in luxury autos, vans, and four-wheel-drive vehicles). General Motors' quality is purely a catch-up strategy, rather than a pull-ahead strategy, and it is chasing rapidly-moving customer expectations and relentless rivals whose quality orientation is to leapfrog over competitors. For instance, the Japanese leapfrogged from low-cost fuel-efficient small cars to quality-engineered, quality-fit-and-finish autos that still offered excellent fuel economy. The result is that General Motors is producing better cars than ever *and* still losing market share. Its management still hasn't grasped the idea that the marketplace sets the quality standard, not the production department at General Motors.

Measuring Customer Expectations: The First Step in Striving for Quality

Delivering products and services that consistently exceed customer expectations requires that companies first understand and measure these customer expectations. Only then can they monitor how satisfied these customers are with their performance and their rivals' performance on the same key dimensions.

A sound approach for assessing expectations of suppliers in any market is to ask customers to identify the key evaluative criteria they use when choosing between suppliers. This is often done by employing rating scales (often termed "multi-attribute attitude scaling") for evaluative criteria. In this way, customers who use different evaluative criteria can be grouped into clusters. Evaluative criteria for small accounts that buy through distributors may vary from those for large accounts that buy direct from the supplier. For example, a small customer who buys a copier or computer from an office equipment dealer may want very fast service on repairs because the customer may not have multiple machines. A larger customer with multiple units may care more about features and price than downtime on a single unit.

Evaluative criteria that are key to supplier selection usually do not exceed six or seven specific items, but these can be chosen from a wide array of factors. Broadly speaking, customers usually evaluate suppliers in six general performance areas. These include:

1. *Overall product characteristics.* These include performance, range of assortments offered, degree of customization available to meet specific customer needs, product packaging, and warranty.

2. *Price.* Included in this category are the payment terms offered, freight policies, minimum order quantities, and the ease with which products can be returned for credit should they prove unsatisfactory for any reason.

3. *Quality of sales force.* Customers consider the company's repair or installation personnel and the availability of technical assistance with product application after sale (to maximize the product's usefulness and solve any problems related to product handling, safety, and operation).

4. *Logistics.* This area encompasses factors such as on-time delivery, responsiveness to rush orders, and the accuracy and speed of order processing, shipping, invoicing, labelling, and order follow-up. Special logistics factors include just-in-time shipping service or the availability of toll-free phone ordering, bar code labels, electronic data entry, shrink-wrapped or special segregated pallets, and advance notice of late shipments or potential back order problems.

5. *Accessibility of support personnel.* These include sales reps, branch offices, headquarters marketers, and repair technicians. Access to support staff is often a separate issue from their quality; it is one thing if a company has an excellent professional sales force but quite another if customers encounter difficulty accessing it when they have a problem. Similarly, repair service quality for equipment can be rated excellent, but repair technician access may be less than ideal. From the customer's point of view, each can contribute to downtime in equipment use.

Figure 6-1. Criteria used by customers in choosing suppliers.

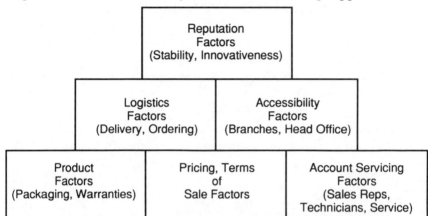

6. *Supplier's overall reputation.* Customers look for financial stability, innovativeness, and product leadership. This overall factor often cannot be tied specifically to evaluative criteria in the other five general areas.

Figure 6-1 diagrams these key evaluation areas that customers consider when making supplier choices.

Different Customers Assign Different Weight to Choice Factors

Customers in different industries vary in how they rank the importance of different supplier factors in contributing to their satisfaction. A major study by Learning International[1] examined what customers viewed as important in vendor selection in seven different industries (high technology, financial services, business equipment, business services, pharmaceuticals, chemicals, and distributor/wholesaler sales). For example, in the business equipment industry, the quality of a supplier's service department was rated as very critical, while this factor was of minimal importance to customers of business services. Chemical company customers considered the problem-solving skills of the supplier's sales reps to be three times more important as did customers of financial services firms. Product performance factors, especially the competitiveness of the offering, mattered most to financial services customers and least to customers of pharmaceutical companies (pharmaceutical customers assume products perform, given the highly regulated nature of this industry). Cross-industry rankings of importance factors showed that three factors contributed almost 75 percent to overall customer satisfaction ratings: dedication to customer service by the supplier's sales reps and their availability and helpfulness in emergencies; the supplier's reputation, financial stability, and caliber of management; and the company's responsiveness to the customer's changing concerns, especially in the area of logistics.

Gap Analysis

Once customers have rated those factors they consider most essential to their satisfaction, a company must then determine from market research feedback how well it is meeting those expectations. One of the best ways to display such data is to use bar charts showing how the company fared on each factor. A line chart can be used to show how competitors are doing. What will show up are gaps between expectation and actual performance ratings. (See Figure 6-2). If the elements of the bar charts are put in descending order of customer importance, the company can visualize at a glance whether its performance gaps are on the most important customer buying criteria or the least important. It can also see whether its competitors are doing better or worse against key buying criteria.

The quality management concept emphasizes using customer expectations rather than competitors' performance to drive quality improvement, since the competition may be performing equally poorly in satisfying customer needs. Nonetheless, gap analysis on both customer expectation shortfalls and competitive shortfalls are very useful in setting priorities for action to improve the company's standing in the customer's eyes. Research at both the University of Florida and Ohio State University[2] shows that, according to customers, the largest gaps in quality occur in logistic services. When logistic shortfalls in areas such as on-time shipments or consistency of delivery occur, companies trying to avoid being caught short of inventory over-order or order far in advance of needs. This excess inventory then must be financed,

Figure 6-2. Customer satisfaction scores—our company vs. the competitor (most to least important).

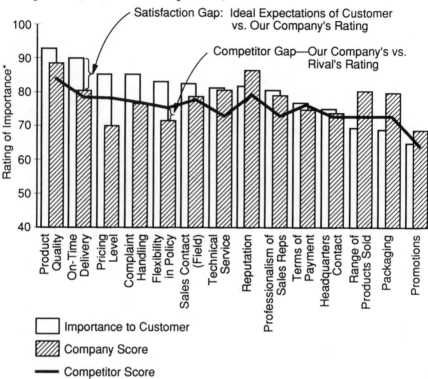

insured, handled, and stored. Inconsistent logistic performance also leads customers to distrust service, so they often double-check invoices and shipments for errors, further increasing their costs.

If a customer experiences a complete stock-out, machinery or even a complete production line may be idled, costing huge amounts of money. Poor logistic support has been found to cause approximately half of all customer complaints,[3] and customer surveys of those characteristics customer value most from suppliers is showing up factors such as "meets promised delivery dates," "avoids long lead times," "fills orders accurately," and "provides advance notice of shipping delays."

Once customer satisfaction "hot buttons" have been identified, suppliers can set performance standards for them. In Germany, BMW offers "service mobiles," mobile service vehicles that are available on call to any customer requiring immediate car repairs.

Customers' needs can vary radically, not just by industry segments but also by geography or culture. For example, product performance is a far more important buying criterion for Japanese households than price, compared to the United States. When Procter & Gamble went to Japan in 1973 to market its leading brands, it assumed that customers in Japan would respond to the same factors that were important to U.S. consumers purchasing disposable diapers, laundry detergents, fine fabric detergents, and feminine hygiene products. This proved to be a very bad assumption. Until 1987, Procter & Gamble lost money in Japan and struggled to boost its sales growth. It had stormed into Japan with U.S. products, U.S. managers, U.S. advertising and promotion, and U.S. sales methods, only to discover that Japanese consumers define "quality" differently than consumers in the United States. So Procter & Gamble altered its products and packaging and got more in tune with what was important to Japanese buyers. For instance, Japanese mothers wanted more "super-absorbent" diapers, sized in smaller sizes than were acceptable in the United States. The result? Procter & Gamble's 1990 sales in Japan topped $1 billion, and the company has the number one brand of product in seven categories of packaged goods.

Marketing's Role in Improving Quality Ratings

As Figure 6-1 shows, the building blocks for customer quality fall into six broad areas. In virtually every one of these six, marketing plays a big role. It is marketing that manages the product line and those factors surrounding the product, from packaging, warranties, and product breadth to the positioning of the product through advertising or personal selling persuasion. It is marketing that has the strongest say in pricing and in setting sales terms and conditions, refund policies, and minimum order levels. Marketing also manages those "people factors" that influence customers, such as the coverage of accounts by reps or key account specialists, technical service personnel, and machine equipment repair technicians.

While marketing is not as directly involved in logistics factors, it is the function that feeds information on customer needs to the supply chain, including the warehouse and factory. Without good feedback from marketing to enable it to put together product forecasts, the factory cannot schedule production. Without accurate marketing forecasts, inventory control cannot make appropriate decisions related to ordering, safety stock levels, and special customer assortment needs required for shipping

Marketing also has a direct influence on the company's reputation. For instance, new product leadership, which directly impacts a company's reputation, is very much a direct responsibility of marketing in conjunction with the research and development function. It is Sony's marketing group that directly influences Sony's overall corporate reputation for innovativeness; similarly, marketing's management of sales resources directly impacts the corporate reputation of companies such as IBM or Merck, widely regarded as world leaders in sales management.

Broad Approaches to Boosting Quality

Once the company has an idea of how its performance ratings compare to customers' expectations (and the ratings of its rivals), it can take several approaches to boosting its quality rating. One approach is to create teams to examine in detail how to correct specific deficiencies in performance or to boost quality to levels that *exceed* customers' expectations by a noticeable margin. This is an engineer's approach to de-bottlenecking problem areas and increasing the differentiating power of factors the company already excels in.

A second approach is to look at factors customers rated as less important than others but on which the company scored well and determine if customers' perceptions of the importance of those factors can be changed, leading to a halo effect for the company. This strategy is being pursued by organizations intent on making their products more environmentally friendly, perhaps because they have a strength in this area compared to their competitors. If the company can convince customers that this aspect of an offering should be more critical in purchase decisions, it can gain share and boost its perceived quality ratings.

In England, for example, Reed Plastic Containers,[4] a subsidiary of Reedpack, has begun marketing a new paint container for paint companies selling to do-it-yourselfers. Reed's paint container is made from see-through, blow-molded plastic and is square with rounded corners. The container is designed with a variety of benefits in mind. The square shape makes the paint container stack better and take up less retail shelf space. The container offers a special brush wiping device and has a special built-in lip so paint can be poured into a roller tray without spilling down the container's side or into the gutter on top, which makes the lid stick on other containers. Because the container is see-through, paint colors are easier to pick out. The handle on the container is designed off-center so that the painter can dip brushes while holding the container without painting his or her own knuckles. The container is recyclable, as well.

In the paint industry, packaging changes have not occurred frequently, so customers don't rate packaging as a key variable in purchasing paint. Yet the introduction of this package by one of Europe's biggest retail paint suppliers, Crown Berger, has boosted Berger's market share by 10–15 percent. In effect, Reed has improved its standing as a supplier by boosting the importance of packaging in the eyes of potential paint customers, despite the fact that packaging design as a factor in vendor selection for paint containers was not very important until Reed's new design showed up in the marketplace.

A third approach to performance gaps in perceived quality is to boost any average ratings for moderately important factors so that they are uniformly excellent. Raising overall quality gives a company's offering more appeal than concentrating only on the most critical customer factor choices. As an example, promotions and product range often show up in customer surveys as relatively unimportant differentiating factors among products. Yet, if a company boosts its performance on these factors from average to excellent, customers notice. For example, Toys "R" Us boosted customer satisfaction and the year-round (as opposed to mostly Christmas) level of toy sales by concentrating on offering customers the widest possible selections and best promotions, even though for many years parents ranked price competitiveness, product availability, and ease of return (if the toy broke or failed) first in importance in their choice of retailer.

Improving Quality Performance in Marketing

Knowing what customers rate as important helps companies focus their efforts on improving quality ratings in the most important customer requirements. But to improve quality significantly, it isn't good enough just to know your score. Companies need to undertake a quality improvement process that emphasizes continuous improvement—in effect a race for quality without a finish line. After all, competitors will improve quality, keeping quality targets in perpetual motion. The components of a sound quality improvement process include:

- Getting the company's marketing leadership committed and involved as missionaries for quality.
- Communicating and tracking data that measure all aspects of quality as it relates to marketing tasks and practices. Continuous customer listening should be the goal.
- Linking quality process initiatives to division and product business plans, as well as efforts to bring key suppliers into the company's quality quest.
- Optimizing human resources so that staff are trained, organized, recognized, and empowered to manage for quality in marketing efforts. This often involves teamwork, flexible assignments, and a push to remove impediments to quality efforts by employees. The company must focus on reducing absenteeism, accidents, turnover, poor morale, and bureaucracy, since these are a drag on the full quality utilization of its people.
- Benchmarking quality results in marketing areas against the efforts of world-class companies considered to have "best practices" in specific aspects of marketing.

Involvement of Marketing Leadership

The marketing leadership in any company cannot pay mere lip service to total quality and expect results. The leadership has to support quality improvement efforts visibly—by talking about such efforts and playing them up with peer executives, customers, and marketing, sales, and customer-service employees.

Leadership must set aggressive quality improvement goals. It should strive to cut the cycle time required to meet customer needs by empowering employees who deal directly with customers to solve problems on the spot wherever feasible. Leadership should seek a flat organization to avoid having customers bog down in bureaucratic delays or confusion. Leaders should be out with customers, seeking feedback on their expectations and how closely these are being met by the total marketing organization. Stanley Gault is a first-class example of visible involved leadership for quality. As Chief Executive Officer at Rubbermaid, he was known as a real "S.O.B. about quality"—whether its product quality, service quality, or quality relationships with key retailers or distributors Rubbermaid relies upon to resell its products.

Committed marketing leadership sets strategic Quality Goals and stresses through words and deeds its belief in the importance of attaining these goals. For example, senior marketing leadership at 3M is trying to cut in half the time it takes to bring new products to market, as part of its commitment to meeting its customers' expectations for product innovation.

The marketing leadership at Xerox stresses Quality in selling by asking all sales personnel and managers to rethink every activity, from paperwork to account management, in order to get sales reps to consider ways to boost customer satisfaction by eliminating work or rethinking tasks that impede or reduce satisfaction. One result of the rethinking process at Xerox has been increased authority in staff hiring, training, and deployment, as well as in pricing, at the district sales office level. This move gave local districts flexibility to improve customer satisfaction by giving them control of key elements affecting customers in their districts.

Leadership among sales executives at Xerox is also changing as Quality Improvement and Customer Satisfaction are stressed. Sales managers are now compensated[5] for improving customer satisfaction, not just for meeting short-term sales forecasts. This compensation change required that sales managers change their emphasis, too. They now must coordinate efforts more closely with service and administration departments, since these groups affect customer satisfaction after sales are made (repairing broken machines or invoicing or authorizing credit).

Bob Galvin, former CEO of Motorola, is an example of a leader who was committed to quality values and who became directly involved in seeing they were emphasized. In 1981, Galvin saw his customers moving to his Japanese competitors, so he set an ambitious goal—a tenfold improvement in product quality by 1986 (in five years). In 1986, he set another goal—a tenfold further improvement in both service and product quality by 1989. He also set a goal of one hundred-fold improvement in quality by 1991 and a goal of six sigma quality for 1992 (six sigma quality is a statistician's way of stating 3.4 defects per million, or 99.99966 percent perfect). And Galvin put his money where his mouth was. He invested $100 million a year in training his people about quality and committed every resource he could to these quality goals. The results are impressive. Motorola won the first Malcolm Baldrige National Quality Award in 1988 and its sales growth in 1990 was up 14 percent over 1989—testimony to how customers respond to higher quality.[6]

"Committed-to-quality" leadership works in almost any endeavour. Ron Dennis, the owner and chief executive of the Formula One auto racing McLaren Team headquartered in Surrey, England, is a man driven by the pursuit of excellence and quality. He has assembled a dedicated team of professionals motivated to succeed. In a business where a Grand Prix team rarely wins more than five or six races in a five- to ten-year period, McLaren is the exception. Since Dennis took over the team in 1982, it has finished either first or second in world standings in 1982, 1984, 1985, 1986, 1987, 1988, and 1989 and has more than 250 cups and trophies in world-class racing.

Tony Andersen, CEO of H. B. Fuller,[7] exemplifies what paying attention to the highest expectations of customers can produce. In 1982, Fuller was an unfocused, broad-line supplier of more than 1,000 adhesives to one hundred different industries. It didn't know its customers' needs well, and its marketing and selling resources were dispersed across too many different product applications. Andersen put a push on to have his 400 sales reps and technical specialists work together and become industry/market specialists knowledgeable about customer needs and sensitive to quality imperatives. Fuller's sales grew dramatically, doubling to $685 million between 1982 and 1988; its stock return to shareholders averaged 26 percent annually in that same period. So quality and focusing on customer needs go hand-in-hand with sales growth, profitability, higher shareholder returns, and—in the McLaren racing team's world—global dominance.

Measuring Quality

Most companies measure and track costs, sales, margins, and other *internally*-derived measurements. *Externally*-derived measures such as customer satisfaction are not regularly measured or even, in some cases, well understood. To commit to quality, a company's marketing and sales personnel must proactively key in on measures of customer satisfaction; without doing so, they cannot take preventive measures to retain and increase sales to these customers.

As a start, external data about customer expectations must be collected and the company's performance benchmarked against these data. In addition, measures internally generated but less closely tied to traditional cost accounting data should be routinely circulated to increase staff awareness and help begin corrective action. Included might be data on numbers and types of customer complaints, customer retention, customer visits by different levels of management, cycle turnaround time for orders, problem-solving call responsiveness, or even something as simple as how many times the phone rings on customer call-ins before someone answers. What doesn't get measured doesn't get managed. For instance, IKEA, the Swedish furniture retailer, continuously measures whether its customer checkout times exceed 10 minutes, because customer feedback consistently ranks waiting time as critical to high satisfaction. A truly conscientious marketing group ought to be measuring progress against customer requirements on all key product and service dimensions.

Failure to measure quality constantly can prove disastrous. In 1986, Carrier Corporation lost touch with its dealer customers and end consumers (contractors) and had a reputation for a "tired" (dated) product line, with poorer quality and order service than its competitors', despite list prices 10 percent higher than those of its rivals. The result was a weakening position with dealers and declining margins, as list prices were discounted to hold unit sales volumes and market share. In 1986, operating margins stood at over 7 percent; by 1989, operating margins had slid to 4½ percent. Carrier decided to mobilize and boost its quality. As a result, by 1990, 75 percent of its sales were from new or redesigned products. But winning back its dealers will prove a longer battle, because repeated equipment breakdowns in the past, despite a quality push today, are not so easily forgotten. Carrier's share[8] of some of its key dealers' sales has slipped by half from its once-dominant 50–70 percent. Had Carrier employed better and regular early-warning measurements of dealer and contractor satisfaction, it would have mobilized much sooner to improve both the design of its products and the inherent quality of its manufacturing processes.

When companies do not measure or even understand what drives customer satisfaction, life can get very complicated. For instance, book publishers do not really understand why bookstores order the books they choose to stock and why some books outsell others. Because of their inability to gauge customer needs, book publishers generously allow book returns from the stores, resulting in return rates for hardcover books of 30–40 percent and for mass-market paperbacks of 50–60 percent. These books are often written off as unsaleable inventory and cost the publishers the production costs of the books. If 50,000 books are returned, costs can escalate to six figures. To understand its customers' needs, Bantam Doubleday Dell, among other publishers, is sending its executives to work in key bookstores, in essence to work "its customer's counters," for two or three days. The company hopes to understand better how bookstores decide to promote the books they do and why certain promotions and displays work. Eventually, armed with this knowledge, it hopes to gauge its retailer-account customer needs more accurately.

Integrating Quality Planning Into Business Plans

Marketing's role in business planning typically involves doing a competitor and market opportunity size-up (market growth, segments, share, penetration, and key accounts), followed by choosing strategies and tactics and assigning responsibilities for action based on the company's strengths and weaknesses.

At a division level, these plans may deal with multiple market or product portfolios; in-depth analysis of demand trends or competitive strategies; or overarching decisions about strategic corporate positioning. Such divisional plans may also include a broad array of substrategies in functions such as manufacturing, purchasing, and research and development, as well as the key concerns of marketing (sales, advertising, distribution, and product-related strategies).

Integrating a Total Quality orientation into this planning system takes place on several fronts. Customers' Quality requirements must be fed into actions to improve quality in functional areas such as manufacturing or product design; for instance, meeting or exceeding customer expectations may require products that are differently designed or made. For instance, Clark Equipment now spends much more time designing forklifts that are more ergonomically sensible and driver-friendly. Seat sizes, noise levels, and operating controls are all designed after extensive research on drivers and driving habits. If the customer's needs are for greater "value" in the product, products may need to be redesigned with a view to cost reduction or feature enhancement. This might mean using fewer parts or more electronics to replace electromechanical components. When Black & Decker really began to improve its products, it found it had to redesign most of its power tools for cordless use and most of its household appliances to add features that customers wanted, such as automatic shut-offs on irons and compactness.

Achieving Total Quality also usually requires that key suppliers become part of the quality improvement effort. This is critical since fully half the cost of manufacturing may be in purchased components or materials from outside suppliers. If suppliers aren't trying to align their quality efforts to the company's, a big part of the total equation will not improve. This idea is also true for service suppliers that work with marketing, such as ad agencies, promotion houses, packaging design firms, and market research agencies. Tighter quality connections with suppliers led Xerox to prune the number of suppliers it dealt with from several thousand to a few hundred. Marketing may wish to "qualify" its ad agencies using a quality audit.

Third, as input from customers about their expectations begins to drive quality efforts in marketing, there must often be significant changes in both tactical emphasis among major marketing spending areas and changes in specific tactics. For instance, a customer survey may tell a company that its basic market offering is considered great, its price value is excellent, packaging and promotions are fine, and its sales force and technical personnel are considered first-rate in all respects. However, customers may also say that the company's logistic fulfilment is inconsistent and unresponsive in emergencies.

The company then has twin challenges. It may need to reorder its overall tactical priorities to spend more resources on logistics within the total marketing mix; it must examine its poor performance in logistics and perhaps modify those systems that aren't delivering the superior service promised by its sales reps. Perhaps it needs to organize more for a just-in-time response or to upgrade the personnel in its shipping warehousing or order entry area. Or perhaps it needs to insist on better service from outside logistics service suppliers (contract warehouses, carriers, customs brokers).

Any policies that get in the way of good service may need rethinking. For example, perhaps the company has been reluctant to let its people work too much overtime, to the detriment of customer service. This policy may need to be changed. Perhaps its inventory rules are too rigid, leading to false savings—that is, it incurs lower carrying costs for stock but faces higher customer defections as back orders occur.

Fundamentally, most business planning winds up considering specific key elements—the market and the company's competitive situation; the company's strengths and weakness; possible strategies; and scheduled tactical actions. What standard size-ups fail to gauge today is the heightened customer concern for quality. This concern must assume a larger role in any plan's situation analysis. Customer quality concerns can lead to a more thorough size-up and provide an additional basis for screening tactical choices. "Engineering" the business plan from the external customer's viewpoint then becomes a vital part of total planning.

Operationally, customer satisfaction ratings become as important as the market research used in the plan to size and segment the market. As a company learns to integrate customer satisfaction into marketing plans, it will eventually have enough confidence to use these data to measure its dealers' performance and shape programs to support them. For example, Volkswagen in Germany ranks its dealers in terms of customer satisfaction reported by those car buyers who have dealt with them. From these assessments, Volkswagen develops the supports its dealers need to better their ratings.

Measuring customer satisfaction can also involve gauging the dealer's satisfaction and from this information developing improved partnering programs. Lyon Metal, an Aurora, Illinois, manufacturer, did extensive research on what its largest industrial distributors wanted and needed in value-added supports. Lyon Metal found it could set itself apart from its rival manufacturers by improving its policies on returned goods and freight allowance and its claims process for goods damaged in transit. Each of these changes saved distributors time or money and led to very productive Lyon Metal partnerships with them.

One of Lyon's distributor partners had this to say about Lyon's efforts to gauge his views of their supports:

> Very few manufacturers understand the problems inherent to the operation of a profitable distributorship. Because Lyon spent the time to find out and incorporate those findings into their policies, we will be able to improve our own bottom-line profits.[9]

Other Issues in Quality

Customer Satisfaction and Product Design

Customer satisfaction ratings can uncover end-user needs that are not being met in current product designs. AB Bahco[10] went to great lengths to research product satisfaction among the contractors and craftsmen who used its screwdrivers. It found that users were dissatisfied with the handle size of most screwdrivers; 70 percent of the time, the handles were too small to permit two-handed use. AB Bahco designed a radically new screwdriver, large enough for two-handed use, with an indentation in the middle of the handle. It marketed its new ERGO screwdriver line very successfully and won an international design award, all because of its extra efforts to improve end-user satisfaction.

It is only through customer probing and listening that such good ideas surface. Fisher-Price's infant car seat has won design prizes because it much more closely meets the needs of new parent customers than do alternative products. The seat can be carried easily from a parking lot and locked securely onto a supermarket shopping cart; it also works as a baby seat for at-home use.

Human Resources: Teamwork, Training, Motivation

Companies that build a quality mind-set into their marketing employ a variety of human resource utilization techniques. They emphasize teamwork in areas where cross-functional teams boost marketing quality; for instance, they may put product managers from marketing, product designers from the lab, and engineers from manufacturing on the same team in an effort to cut time to market for new or redesigned products. Teamwork[11] breaks up a functionally-based organization into a "product–project-based one," enabling the group to perform with less bureaucracy and to set its own pace. It thereby shortcuts communications snafus and turnaround on design revisions, building faster agreement on ways to incorporate customer desires into products while meeting cost/quality parameters *and* acceptable cost/quality standards.

Steelcase, the $1.8 billion office furniture manufacturer, has speeded its throughput in new product commercialization by putting its marketers, designers, and engineers into a teamwork setting. In fact, Steelcase deisgned and built a new $118 million corporate development center to house such project teams at its Grand Rapids, Michigan, headquarters.

Customers are increasingly demanding that companies send

a team that understands the customers' business in order to understand the customers' challenges. The power of teamwork is articulated well in the statement about teamwork quoted in Figure 6-3.

Empowering employees in marketing is another key building block for instilling quality. Marketing employees need both sufficient authority and competence to take actions to satisfy customer needs. Empowerment for quality service goes beyond trusting those employees closest to customers with responsibility and authority. It also requires that management create an atmosphere—via training, recognition, and communication—that enables employees to feel and behave as if they have ultimate control over assisting customers. For instance, the Four Seasons hotel chain has won more awards for distinguished service than any other in North America; in fact, five of the top eight hotels listed by *Institutional Investor* magazine are Four Seasons hotels. The chain achieves these ratings by training employees much longer and more rigorously than other chains; by being tougher in employee selection (for instance, all their concierges must be multilingual); by giving employees the freedom to provide a guest with a complimentary room or meal if a guest is dissatisfied with service; and by stressing maximum communication with and recognition of employees through staff meetings and continuous surveys and suggestions. Four Seasons also pays its employees higher wages than do its rivals, helping keep turnover at half the industry average. Thus it instills pride in employees, retaining the good ones for many years, which provides a solid return on the extra training provided.

Figure 6-3. Teamwork.

Four Brave Men Who Do Not Know Each Other Will Not Dare Attack a Lion.

Four Less Brave Men, but Knowing Each Other Well, Sure of Their Reliability and Consequently of Mutual Aid, Will Attack Resolutely.

> **Colonel Charles Ardant**
> **du Picq (1821–1870)**
> **French Military Scholar**

The power of both forthright communication and perform-
ance-based pay plans to motivate and energize customer-contact
personnel should never be underestimated. For instance, Phil
Bressler, who owns five Domino's Pizza store franchises in Mar-
yland, calculates that regular repeat customers are worth in
excess of $5,000 each over the life of a ten-year franchise agree-
ment. He communicated this $5,000 figure to every order-taker,
delivery person, cook, and store manager, with the result that his
personnel take great care to retain customers by providing exem-
plary customer handling.[12]

Jack Taylor, CEO and owner of Enterprise Rent-A-Car, with
a fleet of 90,000 cars, motivates his employees with monthly
compensation bonuses tied to profits and revenue beyond fore-
cast levels. As a result, Taylor's rental outlet managers often work
extra hours at night and on weekends to ensure that when their
clients need rental cars quickly (Enterprise rents cars primarily to
customers whose cars are in for repair), Enterprise has these cars
prepped and ready for use, despite the last-minute nature of
many customer demands.[13]

Nissan's new Infiniti dealers can qualify for bonuses of
$25,000 if more than 90 percent of car-buying customers buying
from the dealership say they are satisfied when Nissan surveys
them through questionnaires and personal/phone interviews.

Managing Complexity to Improve Quality

Achieving superb customer satisfaction often demands that companies learn to manage their own complexity. For instance, it was
reported in the business press that before Chrysler pruned its
option choices on models such as the Omni, customers faced
more than 8 million possible pricing combinations. By combining
options into standard packages and reducing option choices,
Chrysler cut the number of possibilities to forty-two. When
customers have 8 million choices, a lot of mistakes get made in
manufacturing scheduling, in pricing cars at dealerships, in ordering cars from the factory, in warranty work, in inventorying
part numbers, in advertising materials, and in many other areas
of marketing the product. A marketing emphasis on quality

attempts to minimize complexity so that response time and errors are reduced without unduly restricting customer choice.

Richardson Sheffield,[14] a leading cutlery manufacturer in the United Kingdom, grew from sales of £500,000 in 1975 to £18 million in 1989 by following three simple customer satisfaction rules: All customer letters must be answered the same day they are received; all customer telexes, faxes, or telephone calls must be replied to within the hour of receipt; and all customer requests for samples must be delivered within two days—even on new products.

No exceptions or excuses for failing to obey these rules are acceptable to Sheffield's chairman, Bryan Upton. If there are lots of letters to write or samples to send, employees are expected to stay until the work is done. As simple as these three rules sound, they often result in extra factory shifts and overtime wages—all of which Upton pays very willingly because Sheffield's service has given it outstanding growth and a great reputation for customer service. Upton answers all his own telephone calls from customers personally and does not have a secretary.

Sheffield's growth is all the more impressive considering that total industry growth is declining, while Sheffield's cutlery lines are much broader than ever before, from knives given away in gas station promotions to top-of-the-line chefs' knives costing more than $50 each. Some Sheffield customers such as Sears Roebuck consider their service from Sheffield to be as good as that provided by any of their domestic vendors, despite Sheffield's location 5,000 miles across the ocean.

Whenever things get complicated, the chances for errors or problems increase. Obviously, a quality emphasis that seeks to emphasize zero-defect products or services will wither in an atmosphere of too much complexity. A good case in point is the highly publicized NASA space shuttle flight in which a $1.5 billion space telescope malfunctioned, grounding a flight. The problem was later traced to a small, inexpensive mirror, only one of thousands of parts that wouldn't operate properly. But because every part of a NASA system must work, a small part grounded the flight.

In marketing, reducing complexity can sometimes require developing expert systems to replace complex, time-consuming manual procedures. For example, it used to take a Digital Equipment sales representative between one and three hours to configure systems for customers manually and then write up an order. Digital Equipment has developed expert systems that have reduced product configuration time for difficult systems to fifteen minutes, and the accuracy of rep configurations on orders has gone from 70 percent to 99 percent.[15]

Quality Benchmarking

A company interested in becoming "best of class" in its marketing practices needs to measure its performance against other companies with acknowledged state-of-the-art approaches to specific aspects of marketing.

Figure 6-4 lists world-class companies that stand out in specific marketing operational functions. Benchmarking involves uncovering, in a systematic way, the "secrets to success" of how such world-class companies set functional performance targets and the approaches they use to achieve these high goals consistently. The best companies against which to benchmark are those

Figure 6-4. Acknowledged world-class marketing companies.

Operational Area of Marketing	Company
Product Development	Sony
	Motorola*
Warehousing/Distribution/ Inventory Management	Federal Express*
	Hershey Foods
	The Limited
Market Positioning	Helene Curtis
	IBM
Selling and Sales Management	Merck
	Xerox*
Customer Service/Order Fulfillment	L. L. Bean
	General Electric
Training	Milliken & Company*

*Winner of Malcolm Baldrige National Quality Award

that are top-notch, regardless of industry; businesses can borrow ideas for process improvement from those with leading-edge approaches, even if these approaches are not being used in their industry. In this way, ideas that have been adapted to the company can allow it to leapfrog with quality improvements rather than simply make incremental quality changes.

Benchmarking involves a series of steps, including:

- Identifying which marketing function should get benchmarking priority (selling? logistics? product design?)
- Selecting a company against which to benchmark on that particular function (who's world-class?)
- Getting the target benchmarked company to agree to exchange information by offering a two-way exchange of ideas and data. Gaining this agreement usually involves a letter or phone campaign to the target.
- Putting a six- to eight-person team in place to define the scope of the benchmarking exercise (is it to learn about an entire marketing process or is it just a part of a process, such as a system for order processing or handling incoming telephone orders?) and to flow-chart its own current system (its flaws, output measurements such as cycle time or unit costs, and any recurring problems that seem to crop up).
- Setting up a meeting between the team and the chosen benchmarked candidate. The team should ensure that it has pre-identified the right people to attend and that these people are available to meet on the appointed day. The visit itself often takes a full day. Members of the team may break into small groups with their specific specialist counterparts in order to roll up their sleeves in smaller sessions and explore open-ended questions about different parts of the process with which they are most familiar. Phone numbers and business cards ought to be exchanged for follow-up should other questions occur later on or clarification be required after the team begins to adapt the benchmarked company's targets and process ideas back home.
- Having the benchmarking team put together a comprehensive report comparing its processes to those of the benchmarked partner and then work out priorities for improve-

ment. It may then decide to show its recommendations for its own management to the benchmarked partner. The partner can offer practical guidance and feedback about any potential implementation dilemmas it can foresee with the plan.

This entire process can take several weeks or months from start to finish; since quality process improvements should be continuous, benchmarking often continues over a long period. Benchmarking helps a company really grasp the upper level of performance possible from optimal performance of a specific function and identify the gap between itself and those who are most innovative and productive in this functional area. Alcoa, for instance, has benchmarked administrative, manufacturing, and service functions, which it considers critical to staying competitive as a global aluminum producer.[16] The benchmarking process forced Alcoa to flow-chart and study its own processes. The educational value of this study was almost as good as finding out about others' process strengths in the identical function.

By studying an outsider's way of performing a function, businesses can help their managers get out of the rut of improving on last year's performance by 5–10 percent and can find other companies whose performance of the same function might be 100 or 1,000 percent better than theirs. Xerox, when it undertook its first benchmarking effort in 1980, found its competitors from Japan were so much more efficient at manufacturing that their *retail prices for copiers were often less than Xerox's manufacturing costs per unit*. Xerox discovered that it had nine times more suppliers and seven times more manufacturing defects and that its manufacturing lead times were twice as long. Xerox clearly had to take a whole new look at its product design complexity, its number of vendors, its manufacturing layout, and its supplier delivery service; only then could it get its costs competitive and its quality up.[17]

Many companies' initial experiences with benchmarking have been so enlightening that they have gone on to benchmark many more processes. This is certainly the case at Xerox, which now benchmarks functions such as promotion and public relations—areas far beyond its initial preoccupation with improving manufacturing or customer services. For example, a company that benchmarks IBM's sales force operations might initially be interested in IBM's best ideas and practices in one aspect of sales force management (e.g., hiring and deployment). It might then continue its benchmarking study to examine how IBM manages sales force issues of an administrative nature such as pay plans, expense controls, and sales forecasting.

The Halo Effect of Quality in Marketing

The Marriott Hotel chain illustrates vividly the benefits of having a reputation for marketing and service quality. This hospitality giant ($7.4 billion in 1988 sales) considered building a nursing home containing apartment units in Washington, D.C. In order to determine if there was sufficient demand for such a facility, Marriott did a direct mailing to 45,700 affluent seniors in the Washington area, describing the proposed facility (communal meals, assisted living services, twenty-four-hour emergency call buttons for help). Where most direct mail pieces get a 1–2 percent response rate, this mailing secured 1,806 deposits of $1,000 each to secure priority in apartment selection. All of this was for a facility not yet built or even completely designed! Marriott's reputation for quality in the hotel business is so strong that it created a halo effect on its nursing home business; in fact, its first two nursing home locations, in Virginia and Pennsylvania, had more than 80 percent occupancy from the time they opened, despite the fact that marketing a nursing home is often an uphill battle, since prospects often do not want to recognize their infirmities or face up to the likelihood of becoming infirm in the future.

The Quality Mind-Set

Figure 6-5 summarizes the central tenets of achieving quality in marketing. The outside circle highlights the importance of marketing leadership's commitment to Quality, surveying customer expectations, and preparing Quality plans and Quality teams that can measure Quality results (complaint reduction, higher cus-

Figure 6-5. The processes and priorities that build quality in marketing.

tomer satisfaction, more robust product design). The inner circle underscores the importance of management processes such as front-line marketing personnel empowerment, benchmarking, customer partnerships, and response time improvement.

In their seminal work detailing how Quality in marketing impacts on business and market performance, Bradley T. Gale and Robert D. Buzzell convincingly demonstrate that superior quality goes with superior profitability, growth, and market position.[18] Achieving Quality in marketing is a never-ending quest, because competitors constantly improve and customer expectations shift. What was good enough yesterday may be obsolete today, as demonstrated by the two-thirds of companies cited as "excellent" by Thomas J. Peters and Robert H. Waterman, Jr. (in

In Search of Excellence),[19] that had fallen from grace a few years later.

Problems solved today merely create opportunities to solve new problems created by past solutions. Static prescriptions are not useful in fluid situations. Marketing managements that embrace the need for continuous quality improvement from the customer's perspective stand the best chance of keeping vitality high in their organizations. The key is to build into the everyday attitudes and behaviors of marketing personnel a quality-obsessed mind-set. When this exists, the company stands a very good chance of managing the other core issues discussed in this book, from globalization to innovation to productivity.

Notes

1. *Profiles in Customer Loyalty* (Stamford: Learning International, 1989).
2. Neil S. Novich, "Leading Edge Distribution Strategies," *Journal of Business Strategy* (November–December 1990), pp. 48–53.
3. Ibid., p. 49.
4. "Best Products," *Management Today* (U.K.) (December 1990), p. 65.
5. John F. Tanner, "Leadership Through Quality," *Journal of Personal Selling and Sales Management* (Winter 1990), p. 50.
6. Joseph McKenna, "Bob Galvin," *Industry Week* (January 21, 1991), pp. 12–15.
7. Patricia Sellers, "Getting Customers to Love You," *Fortune* (March 13, 1989), pp. 48–49.
8. Todd Vogel, "Can Carrier Corp. Turn up the Juice?" *Business Week* (September 3, 1990), pp. 78–82.
9. Christine Forbes, "Planned Partnering," *Industrial Distribution* (January 1991), p. 40.
10. "Award-Winning Product Designs," *Industry Week* (November 19, 1990), p. 43.
11. George Stalk, Jr., and Thomas M. Hout, "Competing Against Time," *Research Technology Management Journal* (March–April 1990), pp. 19–24.

12. Frederick F. Reichhold and W. Earl Sasser, Jr., "Zero Defections: Quality Comes to Service," *Harvard Business Review* (October 1990), p. 110.
13. John DeMatteo, "The Company That Jack Built," *Forbes* (October 15, 1990), p. 112.
14. "A Very British Success," *The Economist* (March 4, 1989), p. 66.
15. Dr. Andrew Mitchell, "Expert Systems in Marketing," speech given to Industrial Marketing and Research Association of Canada, Toronto (May 8, 1990).
16. Karen Bemowski, "The Benchmarking Bandwagon," *Quality Progress* (January 1991), p. 24.
17. Seymour M. Zivan, "Benchmarking: The Effective Manager's Tool," *Boardroom Reports* (November 15, 1990), p. 3.
18. Robert D. Buzzell and Bradley T. Gale, *The PIMS Principles: Linking Strategy to Performance*, (New York: The Free Press, 1987), especially Chapter 6 "Quality Is King."
19. Thomas J. Peters and Robert H. Waterman, Jr., *In Search of Excellence* (New York: Harper & Row, 1982).

Index